Championship
Judo

Championship Judo

Mike Swain

EMPIRE Books
P.O. Box 491788, Los Angeles, CA 90049

Disclaimer
Please note that the author and publisher of this book are NOT RESPONSIBLE in any manner whatsoever for any injury that may result from practicing the techniques and/or following the instructions given within. Since the physical activities described herein may be too strenuous in nature for some readers to engage in safely, it is essential that a physician be consulted prior to training.

First published in 2006 by Empire Books
Copyright © 2006 by Empire Books

All rights reserved. No part of this publication may be reproduced or utilized in any form or by any means, electronic or mechanical, including photocopying, recording, or by any information storage and retrieval system, without prior written permission from Empire Books.

First edition
06 05 04 03 02 01 00 99 98 97 1 3 5 7 9 10 8 6 4 2
Printed in the United States of America.

Empire Books
P.O. Box 491788
Los Angeles, CA 90049

ISBN-13: 978-1-933901-17-6
ISBN-10: 1-933901-17-9

Library of Congress Cataloging-in-Publication Data

Swain, Mike, 1960-
  Championship judo / by Mike Swain.
     p. cm.
  Includes index.
  ISBN 1-933901-17-9 (pbk. : alk. paper)
  1. Judo. I. Title.
  GV1114.S93 2006
  796.815'2--dc22

  2006010640

Dedication

I dedicate this book to my parents, Harry and Loretta Swain, who spent countless hours driving me to practice and supporting my Judo career from when I started at the age of 8. They instilled in me the confidence, work ethic and positive attitude it takes to follow your dreams and make them come true.

Acknowledgments

I was fortunate to have so many great coaches, training partners, and friends help me throughout my Judo career. I will always hear the positive voices inside my head of my very first Judo instructor's at age 8, Rick Meola and Tom Seabasty of Judo Tech. Thank you to my long-time coach and mentor Sensei Yonezuka, or Yone, as everyone calls him, from the Cranford Judo and Karate Center, for developing me from a teenage kid into a World Champion and four-time Olympian. Thanks to Alan Coage, Olympic Bronze medalist and ultimate training partner, and all my training partners from Cranford who pushed me to go to Japan and train for the Olympics. Also, thanks to my coach Yosh Uchida at San Jose State University, for providing an excellent training place and, more importantly, making sure I graduated with a degree and moved on in life after Judo. Thank you Sensei Ando and the many Japanese sensei who spent time at SJSU; I could not have progressed without the help of all my coaches, teammates, and training partners at SJSU.

Special thanks to Dan Mistichelli, my college roommate, who made sure I got up and trained on rainy days; Keith Nakasone, the Spartan leader, captain, and close friend, who was always there and encouraging me throughout my career; Coach Willy Cahill for traveling around the world and keeping my body in one piece; and Kimura Sensei and Takagi Sensei of Nihon University in Tokyo, Japan, for giving me the opportunity to train in Japan and treating me like one of the team.

Again, special thanks to my parents for always believing in me and supporting my career.

Last but not least, thanks to my number one coach, my lovely wife Chie, for all of her support while she also had to train for the Barcelona Olympics with the Brazilian Olympic Judo team, and for giving us our two beautiful training partners, our daughter Sophia and son Masato.

Contents

Introduction 12

My Way to Judo 15

CHAPTER 1: Judo Basics

Bowing 30

Ukemi—Falling Techniques 30

Kumikata—Gripping 36

Tai-sabaki (Stance and Body Movement) 38

CHAPTER 2: Throwing Techniques

Throws and Counters 44

Throwing Combinations 66

CHAPTER 3: Judo Grappling

Introduction 92

Gripping Applications 98

Basic Gripping and Turnover Methods 101

Osai-komi-waza (Holding Techniques) 102

Pinning Drills 114

Choking Techniques 121

Championship Judo

Armlock Techniques 135

Grappling Combinations 141

Grappling Turnovers 143

CHAPTER 4: Competitive Judo

Competitive Gripping 148

Transitions to Ground Fighting 166

CHAPTER 5: Training Methods

Warm up and Partner Drills 182

Basic 12-Week Judo Program 192

Judo Band Training 200

12-Week Judo Band Training Program 212

Body Weight Exercises with a Partner 215

12-Week Body Weight Exercises with a Partner Program ... 227

Judo Terminology 230

About the Author 233

Introduction

Championship Judo

Introduction

There is no better feeling than throwing your opponent to the ground effortlessly with a foot sweep or hip throw before they had even known you had attacked. In fact, a perfect throw happens so fast that even the person executing the throw will get right up and forget what happened for a split second. That is called an ippon or perfect throw in Judo. An ippon happens only when your mind, body, and spirit all work together in one flash of a moment.

Championship Judo is about the techniques, training methods, drills and curriculums of modern-day Olympic Judo. The original Kodokan Judo, founded back in 1882 by Professor Jigoro Kano, encompassed many other techniques and kata that are important for the understanding of overall Judo as a self-defense, but often are left out in the quest for Olympic medals. My intention in writing this book is not to create the encyclopedia of Judo but to give you a more direct view of the techniques applied today in Judo competitions around the world.

I have had the privilege of training and competing on four Olympic Judo teams: 1980, 1984, 1988, and 1992, as well as coaching the 1996 Olympic team and training and competing in five World Championships: 1977, 1983, 1985, 1987, and 1989. These experiences have taken me around the world and given me in-depth, real-life competitive and training knowledge of modern-day Judo. This is what I wish to pass on to you through this book.

A good solid basic knowledge of how the techniques of modern Judo work are key to the development of all Olympic caliber athletes. Therefore I have broken down the important basic techniques of Throwing, Holding, Chokes and Armlocks into 1, 2, and 3 step-by-step learning blocks for easy understanding and teaching. Each technique may have one or two variations for competition, but it is critical that one understands the basic movement before trying to learn a fancy variation.

Judo techniques are a combination of standing throws or takedowns and grappling on the ground with Submissions. Grappling can be learned quicker and easier because you can move at your pace at a more controlled speed, whereas throwing takes much more timing with more complex movements, as well as knowledge of how to fall in order to prevent injuries. However,

Introduction

Judo can be learned by all ages and at all ages; it is just a matter of learning at your own pace. Judo helps your mind and body to work together and creates a very calm feeling that is hard to match after a good workout.

Championship Judo is a book for everyone to enjoy. The novice judo practitioner will find a simple explanation of the basics that can give one a leg up on getting started. The advanced player can pick up on small, yet important, details that will improve one's techniques and provide a competitive edge. The book is filled with many drills and alternative curriculums using training bands and functional body weight exercises that can be used at all levels.

Enjoy!

Mike Swain

My Way to Judo

by Mike Swain

My judo career started in 1968. I had no idea I would become a four-time Olympian, let alone the first man from the Western hemisphere to win the World Judo Championship. I was 8 years old and my uncle Jim's military buddy Richard Meola, a former drill sergeant in the U.S. Marine Corps, was opening up a new judo school. My uncle explained to my parents that judo would instill me with confidence, discipline, and focus. My parents were convinced and they agreed to let me join Mr. Meola's school.

I remember the first day of class very clearly: Sensei (teacher) Tom Seabasty, who was Mr. Meola's partner in business, handed me my first judo uniform and white belt. The uniform smelled nice, like fresh cotton. Sensei Seabasty then explained the two facets of Judo philosophy to me: he told me about the use of maximum efficiency with minimal effort, and about the concept of mutual welfare and benefit. He told me that judo is a Japanese word meaning "the gentle way" and that Jigoro Kano founded the Kodokan, the first judo dojo ever, in 1882.

He also explained the importance of giving and receiving respect. I learned that bowing to my sensei and to my partner was a way of showing and receiving respect. Everything was new and I was very nervous, but Mr. Seabasty made me feel comfortable and introduced me to lots of other classmates.

Three months later, I competed in my first tournament, the Junior Olympics, a big event for a first timer. I was able to place fourth. This earned me a medal and gave me a lot of confidence.

When I was 14, Sensei Meola suddenly died of a heart attack. He was only in his early thirties and his death was unexpected. This was sad and shocking news for all of his students and their parents because he was well loved by all of them. They loved his strong character, marked by discipline and a tenacious fighting spirit to win. He also was an inspiration to me personally: he once wrote me a letter—a letter I still have today—that said he was sure I would become a great champion in judo.

Since the beginning of my judo career, a part of Meola sensei has always been there with me on the mat.

Championship Judo

1985 World Finals, Seoul, Korea, Swain (USA) vs. Ahn (Korea)

1985 World Finals, Seoul, Korea, Swain (USA) vs. Ahn (Korea)

Two years later, I won my first National Championship. This marked the beginning of a long and successful judo career for me.

In order to take my judo to the next level, I joined the Cranford Judo & Karate Center, which was founded by Mr. Yoshida Yonezuka. Also known as "Yone," he was Mr. Meola and Mr. Seabasty's original Sensei.

Yonezuka Sensei immigrated to the United States from Japan in the early 1960s. He was an incredible judo champion in Japan and was the strongest judo fighter in the USA at the time. Yone, who taught by example, worked out with everyone every night, and was able to tremendously improve my Judo technique in just a few years. When I was only 16 years old, Yonezuka Sensei coached me to win the World Championships Trials. I was the youngest U.S. World Team member ever.

The next year I traveled to Japan to compete in the 1978 Jigoro Kano Cup, my first international event. At the time, Japan was preparing for the 1980 Olympics and fielded a superstar team of four competitors in each weight class. This event was probably the toughest Judo event I have ever competed in to this day. The atmosphere was epic: it took place on a single raised mat in Budokan Hall, the historical home of the Olympic Judo competition in 1964. The Japanese all-stars dominated the field, winning six of seven gold medals. The competition was so fierce that I won only one match that day, which was one better than any American at the event!

The Kano Cup was a turning point in my career: it introduced me to the world of Judo and changed my mindset toward training. It motivated me to train harder when I returned to America.

When I got back home, I was intent on training harder than ever before. I knew I was at the right place because Cranford Judo Club was well known for its tough judo fighters. One of the toughest was 1976 heavyweight Olympic bronze medalist Alan Coage. Alan was my mentor and made sure that I worked out 150 percent every day. (This included him throwing me mercilessly night after night after night!) Alan saw my potential and suggested that I train for the 1980 Olympics by moving to Japan after high school.

I took his advice and received a letter of recommendation from Yonezuka Sensei.

Next came the hard part: convincing my parents that going to Japan fresh out of high school was the right thing to do. At the age of 18, I sold my first car (which at my age was a real hard thing to do) and started working over the summer to save money.

My parents finally agreed, albeit reluctantly, to let me go to Japan when I told them I had a friend there who would pick me up when I got to the airport. The reality was that I didn't know anybody in Japan and that the one contact I did have never received my letters asking for help.

Nevertheless, I bought my ticket and left for a foreign land with no contacts and no idea of what would happen.

When I arrived in Japan, alone and with little money, I was nervous and excited. I also realized that I couldn't speak or read any Japanese!

1985 World Finals, Seoul, Korea, Swain (USA) vs. Ahn (Korea)

1985 World Semifinals Swain (USA) vs. Blach (Poland)

For the first few weeks, I lived at the Kodokan and trained twice a day there. Eventually, I met up with my original contact and moved into a temporary apartment near Nihon (also known as Nichi Dai) University, which was the school that my sensei Yonezuka graduated from.

I remember my first day of practice at Nichi Dai University. Head instructor Kimura Sensei was having special winter training sessions that week. I woke up at 4 a.m. and saw six inches of freshly fallen snow on the ground outside. I then hopped on my bike for a freezing 20-minute ride to the Dojo. A policeman stopped me along the way—I think he thought that I had stolen the bike, but since I spoke no Japanese I had no way to explain. Since I didn't know what else to say, I immediately uttered the words "Kimura Sensei," in an effort to explain where I was going. Upon hearing the name, the police officer immediately let me go with no further questions. I continued on my way to practice, surprised at my good fortune and later found out that Kimura Sensei was actually in charge of the Tokyo Police Judo Team!

The training at Nichi Dai was insanely difficult. It was so hard that I cannot explain it in words. One would have to have experienced this training to understand how it feels. I experienced levels of body soreness and physical pain that were previously unknown to me.

It was mid-winter and Kimura Sensei

purposely ran practice with all of the windows open; if you stood still, you would freeze.

Because of the cold, the mats felt like cement.

There were no weight classes at Nichi Dai and most of the fighters were 40 pounds heavier than me—I weighed a mere 160 pounds at the time. These large men fought ferociously because they were training to make the college team, which consisted of the best seven players at any weight.

Because of my size and the intensity with which the Japanese team fought, I found it hard to catch anyone with big throws. I was forced to rely on my speed and technique in order to survive. Because of this, I was able to raise my ashiwaza (or foot sweeping techniques) to a new level, and eventually used it to win many championships.

At Nichi Dai, there was nowhere to hide in the dojo; if you weren't working out, everyone could see you. One day, I was slow to grab a partner and Takagi Sensei, a former world light heavyweight champion and future coach of Nichi Dai, yelled at me in Japanese. "Jibun de sure," he growled. I understood little Japanese, but I intuitively knew what he was saying. He was telling me that in order to become a champion I had to do it myself, not wait for others to help me.

The techniques I learned and, more

Gold Medal, World Championship, 1987
Essen, Germany

Championship Judo

Swain, USA, vs. Koga, Japan
1987 World Championship, Essen, Germany

Swain, USA, vs. Alexander, France
1987 World Finals, Essen, Germany

importantly, the fighting spirit I felt while sweating, training, and battling with so many great fighters and coaches at Nichi Dai contributed greatly to the success I had in judo competition. Not only that, it also contributed to the development of my overall character.

When I returned from Japan in late 1979, I received a call from Mr. Yosh Uchida, founder and coach of San Jose State University Judo. I knew that San Jose State was undefeated for 20 years in collegiate Judo and had the strongest team in the USA. Mr. Uchida's program married judo and academics perfectly and I was able to train and attend classes at the same time. I decided to attend San Jose Sate University on a partial scholarship, and focused on making the 1980 Olympic team and starting school.

I soon met and became friends with Keith Nakasone, whom I had previously seen at the Jigoro Kano Cup. The first time I saw Keith at State, he was practicing with a cast on his leg! He had just come off of knee surgery but was still working out because he seriously wanted to win the 1980 Olympic trials. (We both went on to win the trials in 1980.) The sight of Keith practicing in his cast reassured me that I had made the right choice: the fighting spirit I had seen in Japan was also at San Jose State.

Uchida sensei also had a strong spirit. He had a hard-line policy about making good grades and would read everyone's grades out loud in order to embarrass anyone who performed poorly and—though he would never admit it himself—praise anyone who excelled. It was important to him that we all graduate and become successful in life, not just win judo medals. Though I didn't understand it at the time, I later came to appreciate Uchida sensei's focus on academics. When I graduated from SJSU, I became part of a winning tradition, a family of alumni that would help me both in competition and in life after competition.

After winning the Olympic trials in 1980 at the age of 19, I was ready to fight and win. Unfortunately, this did not happen:

*Mike Swain & Yosh Uchida
San Jose State University*

*Mike Swain and Coach Yone Yonezuka,
Tokyo, Japan*

Meola Sensei

Nihon University—Tokyo, Japan

Training at Tokyo Police Academy

the U.S. boycott of the 1980 Olympics was very frustrating for me, but it was devastating for all the Olympians competing for the last time. (Ironically, the USA would invade Afghanistan 20 years later for the same basic reasons it condemned the USSR.)

Instead of discouraging me, the 1980 Olympic boycott fueled me to train harder, and I began to win internationally, something few Americans could do at the time. Between 1980 and 1984, I competed and trained in many European countries and gained lots of confidence and experience along the way. The 1984 Olympics came quickly and the fact that they were held in Los Angeles added to my already high pressure to win. In the end, I did not medal but made a good showing: I lost a close match to Bronze medalist Onamura from Brazil, the same man I would easily defeat two years later for the Gold medal at the 1987 Pan American Games.

The year 1985 marked another stepping stone in my career. I became the first American man to win a silver medal at the world championships in Seoul, Korea. In the final, I fought and lost a tough match against Olympic Gold medalist Ahn from Korea. As I walked off the mat that day, all I could think of was how close I had come to winning the gold. I was not happy with silver and began to wonder if I could train any harder, and if it would make any difference if I did. I will always remember these thoughts: I fought against them in my mind and came to the conclusion that I must never, ever give up.

In 1986, I would run into a much bigger roadblock: Koga. He was a young, dynamic

Dutch Open 1982

Czechoslovakia Open 1982—Prague

*Mike and Chie Swain
1992 Olympics, Barcelona, Spain*

Swain Family, San Jose, CA

*Swain Family in Sao Paulo, Brazil
Luiza Ishii, Chiaki Ishii (1972 Olympic Medalist), Swain Family, Vania Ishii (2000, 2004 Olympic Team Brazil)*

fighter who was beating all the superstars in Japan at the time. I remember fighting him in the finals of my third Kano Cup. I underestimated him and his explosive throws because I had fought and beaten top Japanese fighters before. I lost by a full ippon halfway through the match. This loss tested my faith in myself again. I decided that I needed to focus more on my conditioning.

I decided to go to Kendal, England, to train with world champion Neil Adams and his coach Tony McAllen. Tony and I connected right off the bat and I was reintroduced to some good old-fashioned hard training.

While I was in England, I trained with many top athletes, including Olympic champion and human training machine Robert Vandewalle. Robert was a real physical specimen and was a maniac in the gym. He motivated me to push myself farther than I had ever imagined before. We focused on increasing my physical conditioning through weights, running, and sport-specific technique.

While in London, I also met Kashiwazaki, another world champion from Japan. He helped me to refine my sumi-gaeshi, a takedown that would eventually help me to win the world championships.

After two months of intense physical conditioning in the UK, I went back to Japan for some final hard-core training with the Tokyo Police and Nichi Dai University, among others. I had lost the Worlds before, but this time I was focused and determined to win for myself.

In 1987, in Essen, Germany, I made history by winning the World Championships and defeating my rival Koga along the way. My proud coach was Yone, who had molded me at a very young age and watched me grow into a world champion.

I remember being in a fairly relaxed mood that day. I let my body and mind go into remote control, never doubting myself that I would win. Although I would later go on to win Olympic Bronze in 1988 and a silver medal in Belgrade, Yugoslavia, in 1989, the 1987 Worlds was my best performance, my crowning achievement.

In 1992, I competed in my last tournament at the Barcelona Olympics, where I was accompanied by my wife Chie, who competed in Judo for Brazil. I had broken my rib a few months before and my training was limited, so I did not do well, but being there with my wife was a very special event.

1980 Boycott with President Carter at the White House

1980 Olympic Judo Team

Championship Judo

*1984 Olympic Judo Team
Los Angeles, CA*

In the end, I understand more clearly the philosophy of Judo that was explained to me when I was 8 years old. "Maximum efficiency with minimum effort" means to constantly perfect your physical and mental techniques to become more efficient, to pare everything down so that there is no waste when you take an action. "Mutual welfare and benefit" means to take care of your partner and community so everyone benefits and grows along with you. Judo has taught me to win humbly and lose graciously.

But the biggest things I have learned from Judo—from all the training and traveling, trials and errors, victories and defeats—are belief and faith. I learned to believe in my dreams and to have faith in myself. It is easy to persevere when you win; but in life, as in Judo, you will be thrown down and you will fall many times. Sometimes the falls are hard, but it is what you do from that point—the point after the fall—that counts. You must always get back up and move on, never settling for second best.

I have had so many training partners, teammates, coaches, and friends who have supported me on the way that it is impossible to name them all. To everyone, I say thank you for all your help. I'd like, however, to give a special thank you to my two biggest fans: my parents, Harry and Loretta Swain.

Thank you for supporting me from the beginning and for teaching me to always do my best.

1988 Olympic Judo Team
Seoul, Korea

1992 Olympic Judo Team
Barcelona, Spain

Chapter 1

Judo Basics

Bowing

Bowing should be the first part of any judo class. As in many martial arts, the bow in judo is a symbol of respect. There are two basic ways to bow:

Standing—Begin by standing with your back straight and your heels touching. As you bow, move your hands to the front of your legs.

Kneeling—Begin by bringing down your left leg first, then your right. Position your knees approximately two fists apart. Place your hands in front of your knees, pointing toward each other at a 45° angle. A rear view of the kneeling position shows that

the left toe is tucked underneath the right toe. In completing the bow, place your hands on your inner thighs and straighten your back.

Ukemi—Falling Techniques

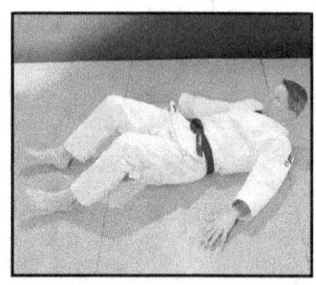

Falling techniques are the essence of judo. Teaching your students how to fall may be the most important thing you teach in judo. Ukemi lays the foundation not only for the safety of the student, but also for the student to go on to learn more complex techniques.

The first part of learning ukemi involves becoming comfortable with the mat. Lie on your back with your head up and your knees slightly bent. Slap the mat using the soles of your feet. Next, slap the mat at a 45° angle with your palms down. Then together, slap the mat with your hands and the soles of your feet at the same time.

Judo Basics

Rear Break Fall

Start in a sitting position with your chin tucked in and your hands out in front. Then roll back and slap the mat with the palms of your hands, arms outstretched at a 45° angle. As you slap the mat, your feet come up. Remember to breathe out as you are falling back.

Rear Break Fall from a Squatting Position

Balance yourself in a squatting position with your arms out. Roll back, keep your chin tucked in, and do not reach back to slap the mat. Your legs should come up freely as you roll back and slap the mat.

  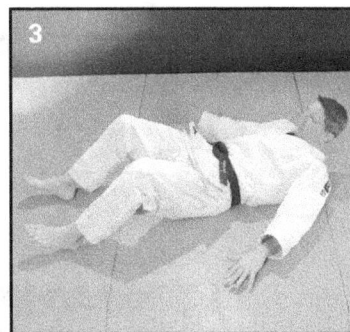

Championship Judo

Squatting Clap Exercise

This exercise is good for beginners whether they are children or adults. Facing a partner, stand with your legs shoulder width apart. Squat down and put your hands out in front of you. Together, you push into each other with your hands, and then roll back and slap the mat. Next, try it in a diagonal direction. Make sure your elbows do not touch the mat before your hands. This exercise teaches timing and proper technique.

Side Break Fall—TV position

The proper position for this fall is similar to lying on the couch while you are watching television. Start by placing the palm of your hand 45° away from your body. The knees should be slightly bent. The left foot should slap with the sole of the foot. Your right foot should slap on the top of the foot. Slap your hands and your feet at the same time.

Judo Basics

Side To Side Slap the Mat

Next, go from left to right. The most important thing is not to let your feet cross over. Lift your hips off the mat and twist your body slapping with your left hand then your right hand.

 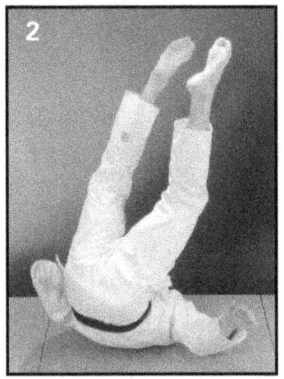 

Side Break Fall from the Squatting Position

Maintain a wide stance in order to keep your center of gravity as low as possible and squat as low as you can. Place your hand underneath your elbow to keep your arms straight with your palm down. You want your hands to slap the mat before your elbow. As your foot slides across, your body falls, and your hand slaps the mat. Your hips should touch the mat first followed by the palm of your hand. If you bend your elbow, you will injure your shoulder. After you feel comfortable with the right side, switch to the left side. This is a difficult position for beginners. Make sure they maintain a wide stance and keep their elbows straight.

Forward Break Fall

Start on your stomach with your hands in front of you. Slap the mat several times just to get the feel for the mat. Next, from the kneeling position, fall forward and slap the mat with your hands in front of your face. It's very important that your hands break the fall instead of waiting for your body to touch the mat. From the standing position, relax your body, fall forward and slap the mat before your body touches it.

Forward Break Fall from Knees

Forward Roll

Let's start with a basic forward roll or forward tumble. With your head tucked in directly between your legs, stay in a ball and roll forward coming up onto your feet.

 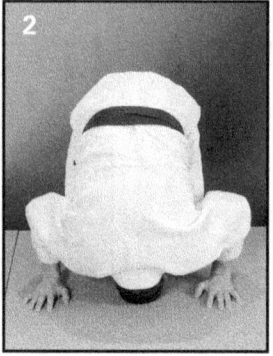 

Judo Basics

Forward Judo Break Fall from Knees

The difference between the forward judo break fall and the basic forward roll is that you roll over the shoulder and not straight forward as is done in the basic forward roll. Start from a kneeling position. If you are going to roll from the right side, place your right hand forward first. Roll on your right shoulder and slap the mat with both your hands and legs. Push off with your left foot while turning your head to the left. It is important to finish in the proper position: slapping at 45°, legs not crossed and head off the mat.

 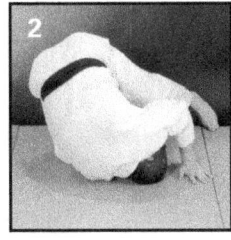  

Forward Judo Break Fall from Squat

Next, let's try it from a squatting position. All things are the same except you start from a squat. Land in the side position.

Forward Judo Break Fall from Standing to Standing

Start in standing position and roll back to your feet. This time you're going to come up from the roll with your feet shoulder width apart. The most important part is in the finish where you slap the mat as you finish the roll.

Kumikata — Gripping

The Classic Grip — Sleeve Hand

The key to off balancing your opponent lies in mastering kumikata. The most important aspect of gripping is pulling your opponent off balance with the sleeve hand. Grip the sleeve with the bottom three fingers of your hand. The pinkie finger is the strongest point. Your forefinger and thumb should lie relaxed on top of the sleeve material. As you pull, turn your pinkie up and turn your head. This tightens the grip and makes your opponent come further off balance enabling the throw. If you pull your opponent towards you without turning up your pinkie, your opponent will not step forward.

The Classic Grip — Lapel Hand

Next, grip the lapel tight with your first three fingers starting with the pinky; keep your thumb and forefinger relaxed. With your pinkie finger facing down, snap your wrists back. Your elbows should be relaxed. An easy way to remember this is to picture yourself fishing. As you catch a fish, you snap your wrist back to pull the fish out of the water. This is the same motion, or action, that your lapel grip takes. The more relaxed your grip, the faster you will be able to pull your opponent forward.

Judo Basics

Gripping Exercise

A simple and basic training exercise to increase strength and train your fingers for the correct gripping movement is the open hand grip. Practice by having the class stand in a circle with hands and arms out. Each person should count to ten, progressing to 100-500 based on the experience of the group. Make sure each time they grip the pinkie finger closes first.

Here are some other types of grips

1. Lapel to lapel—gripping both lapels.

2. Around the neck—grabbing the back of the collar in one hand and the sleeve in the other.

3. Grip underneath the arm and around to the belt.

Remember, if you grip the belt, you must attack within three seconds.

4. Over arm.

Tai-sabaki (Stance and Body Movement)

In judo, posture is very important in controlling and throwing your opponent. A good posture is when your whole body is relaxed, feet are parallel to each other and pointing slightly inward, knees are slightly flexed with legs about shoulder width apart, hips should be back and shoulders relaxed, but alert. There are three basic stances: Natural or straight with feet parallel; left with the left foot facing forward; and right with your right foot facing forward.

Defensive Stance

For a more defensive stance just lower your core body or hips.

Offensive Stance

For a more offensive stance, move your body closer and pull your opponent in.

Judo Basics

How your posture affects balance: When your opponent is bent over, it is very easy to pull him forward or push him backward. However, when he stands straight up with his legs parallel apart, it's difficult to off balance him. Keep your body posture straight up, your knees and elbows slightly bent. Always try to stay in front of your opponent. The key is to be relaxed and not let your opponent feel your strength. As your opponent tries to move, move with him and out of his way. Do not try to meet his power directly head on. The most important thing in an effective attack and defense is to concentrate 100% and always remain relaxed.

Push-Pull Theory

If an opponent is pushing against you, you pull him off balance by using his own force against him. And, when your opponent is pulling you, your reaction is to push, or attack, forward using his strength against himself to push him off balance. The Push-Pull Theory is the fundamental theory behind judo.

Push

Pull

Posture and Relaxation:

Posture and relaxation is also very important in judo, in both attacking and defending. Most beginners will start with stiff arms making it very easy for them to be pulled off balance. The key is to relax and bend your elbow, therefore making your body even more flexible and harder to pull off balance.

Stiff posture

Relaxed posture

Eight Directions for Off Balancing
Backward

Forward

Both sides

Judo Basics

Diagonally forward to both sides

Diagonally backward to both sides

Three Main Components of All Throws

Closely watch the position in which you put your opponent as you force him off balance. After you put him into this position, there is one more step and that is simply following through with, or executing, the technique. The three basic elements in creating a technique are off balancing, positioning and follow through.

Off balancing   *Positioning*   *Finish*

Chapter 2

Throwing Techniques

Throws and Counters

Hiza-garuma (Knee wheel) Kneeling position

Start with your opponent on both knees. Hold onto both of his sleeves with your bottom three fingers, grasping tightly with your forefinger and thumb relaxed. In this throw you are going to spin your opponent around in circles by placing your foot right against his knee and then moving out of his way. Your body must move to the side in order for him to move forward. Your pulling arm pulls up and your other arm spins him around. As you're spinning, turn your head and look the other way. This is also an excellent exercise in teaching the student how to slap the mat. Start with pulling the sleeve and then try with the lapel hand first. Be careful with lapel hand pulling, make sure the opponent keeps their slapping hand on your sleeve until they turn to their back to slap. This is important to learn in order not to injure their arm when they practice from a standing position.

Sleeve pull

Lapel pull

Throwing Techniques

Hiza Garuma—From a standing position

It's recommended that you use a landing pad when you are teaching beginners this throw. The first thing to do is pull forward with lapel hand and hop to the side. By hopping to the side, you reinforce the fact that you must move to the side for the throw to work. If you stay in front of your opponent, you will stop the throw. As you step to the side, make sure you pivot your foot. This allows you to follow through with the throw. As you step back and to the side, your opponent steps forward. This is the moment in which you place your foot on his knee.

Front view

Defense against Hiza Garuma

The basic posture is to lower your core area and point your foot outward, taking a slightly wide stance. Then counter with your own Hiza garuma to the opposite side.

O-Goshi (Full Hip Throw) Front

O-goshi is an excellent throw for beginners to learn, because it encompasses all the basic movements of hip throws. I will explain two entries, direct front enter and side enter.

Direct front enter: The first point is to pull your opponent off balance with your sleeve grip. Step directly in the middle of his two feet with your lead foot or the foot opposite your pulling hand, (if you are pulling with the right hand then step with the left foot) and reach around the back about belt level. While reaching around, bend your knees and keep your back straight. Next, turn your hips and body stepping back with the other foot. Your feet should be shoulder width apart. Make sure your center of gravity is underneath your opponent's belt line, pick up using your knees with back straight, and throw. It's important that you pull your opponent off balance before you try to pick him up.

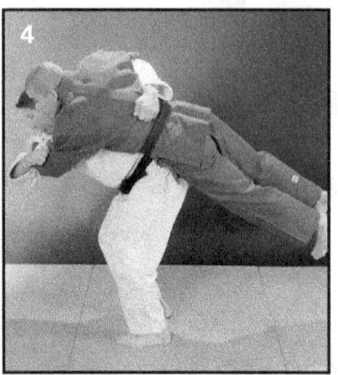

Throwing Techniques

O-Goshi (Full Hip Throw) Side

Follow the same basic steps as in the direct front enter, except instead of stepping directly in the middle of your opponent's feet, you should step to the outside of his feet first and pull him close to your body, then step in front and shoot your hip across for the throw.

Basic Point of Attack

As in all judo throws, the basic point of attack is from the top of the triangle. The top is between your opponent's legs and out as far as his feet are apart. This is where you pull him off balance. If you try to pull him from the side, his defense will stop your body from turning. This is the point where most beginners will get stuck. Therefore, go back to the top of the triangle, pull your opponent off balance, pick him up and finish the throw.

Defense Against O-Goshi

The counter to O-goshi is O-goshi. As your opponent attacks, stop him by dropping your core and maintaining posture, move to the side and slide your hips in front of him to apply o-goshi.

47

Championship Judo

Osoto-Gari (Outer Leg Reap) Standard

Holding with a standard grip, pull your opponent off balance with your lapel hand while stepping in with opposite foot. As you step forward, your leg comes through and chops out his rear leg ("gari" means to chop or cut). It's important that you use this action against his leg. As you move forward, use your whole body like a pendulum to throw him. The basic throw is broken down into 4 steps.

1. Pull and step with opposite foot

2. Pull sleeve hand out twisting pinky up, pull lapel hand in (snapping wrist up) and step next to opponent's foot.

3. Push through with lapel hand and kick up

4. Bring leg down pointing toe and finish throw. Your head and leg must go down together.

Throwing Techniques

Osoto-Gari (Outer Leg Reap) Opponent Steps Back

The correct timing for osoto-gari is when your opponent steps back, you step forward. In order to make him step back you must pull forward. As he reacts and steps back, you follow the step with your foot right next to opponent's rear foot. Make sure your body moves forward as your opponent moves back to create the correct timing and off balance to throw with ease.

Defense Against Osoto-Gari

There are two basic defenses.

1. As opponent comes into the attack, place your foot that is attacked firmly on the mat. Then take a deep step back and to the side. Continue to turn all the way into Osoto-gari.

2. As opponent tries to chop at your lead leg, simply relax your leg and hip sliding your leg to the outside. Then pull your leg back as far as possible and go back to the basic judo posture.

Championship Judo

Ippon Seio Nage Basic (Shoulder Throw)

Classic forward throw from the Tewaza category or hand technique. Forward off-balancing is done with both hands/wrists snapping forward and pulling your opponent. Position your body by turning 180 degrees, keeping your back straight and bending at the knees. Follow through by bending forward at the trunk, extending knees and coming onto your toes all at once. Seio Nage is best applied by a shorter player against a taller opponent. It's critical to pull and lift up with the sleeve hand on the pulling arm to bring your opponent onto her toes or when your opponent is pushing into you.

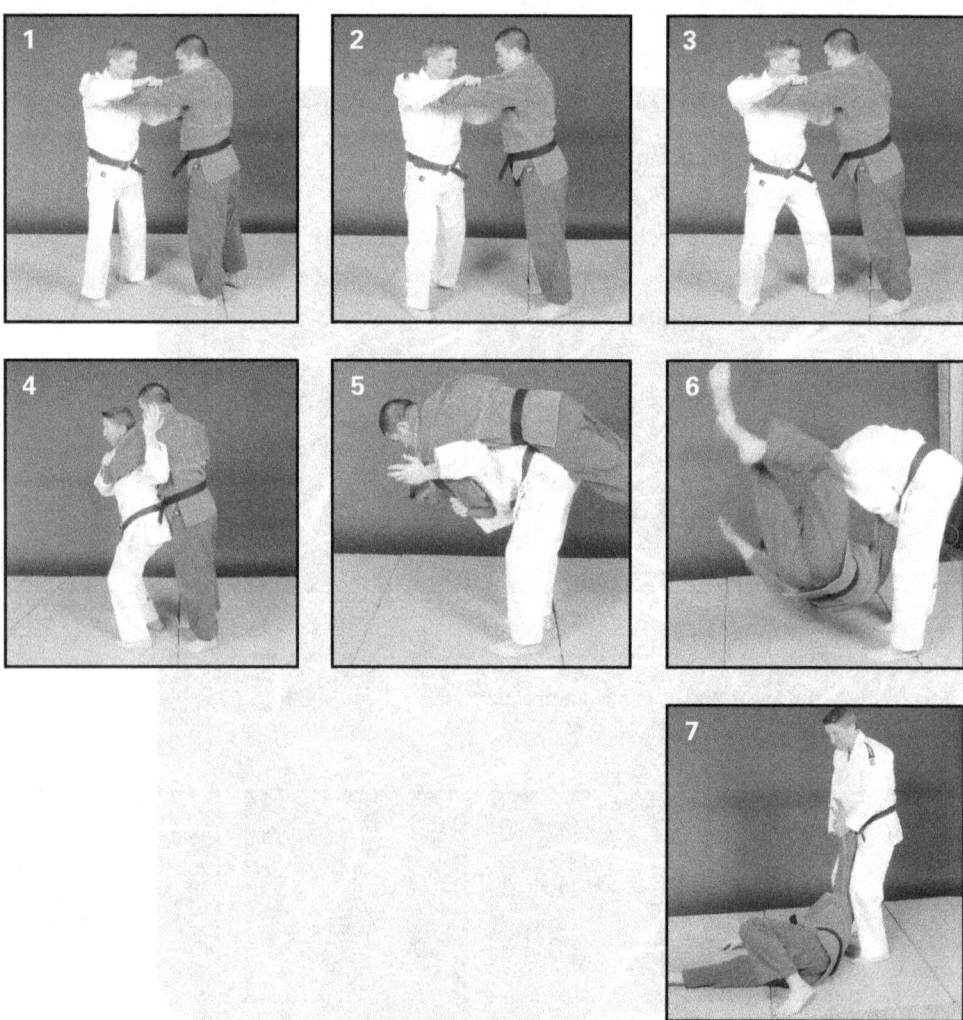

Throwing Techniques

Ippon Seio Nage Variation #1 (Pull Forward to Off-Balance)

In this variation try to pull your opponent forward and make him take a step. As your opponent's weight distributes onto his forward foot, pivot and enter. By keeping your feet closer together you can pivot quickly and get into position. Your belt should be lower than your opponent's in order to get underneath his center of gravity. Lock the shoulder tight, keeping your opponent's arm away from your neck. Rotate your core and throw your opponent directly in front of you.

 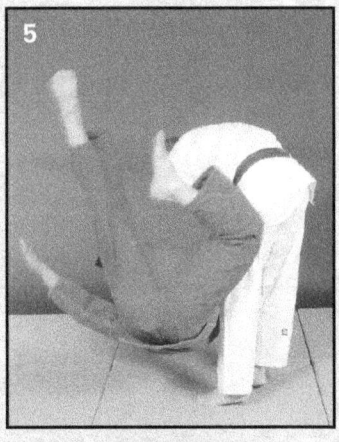

Championship Judo

Ippon Seio Nage Variation #2 (Pull From Lapel)

Hold the lapel instead of the sleeve. Use the lapel to off-balance your opponent by pulling forward and up. The lapel is effective because there is less slack in the material and you can control your opponent's body better. The remainder of the throw is the same.

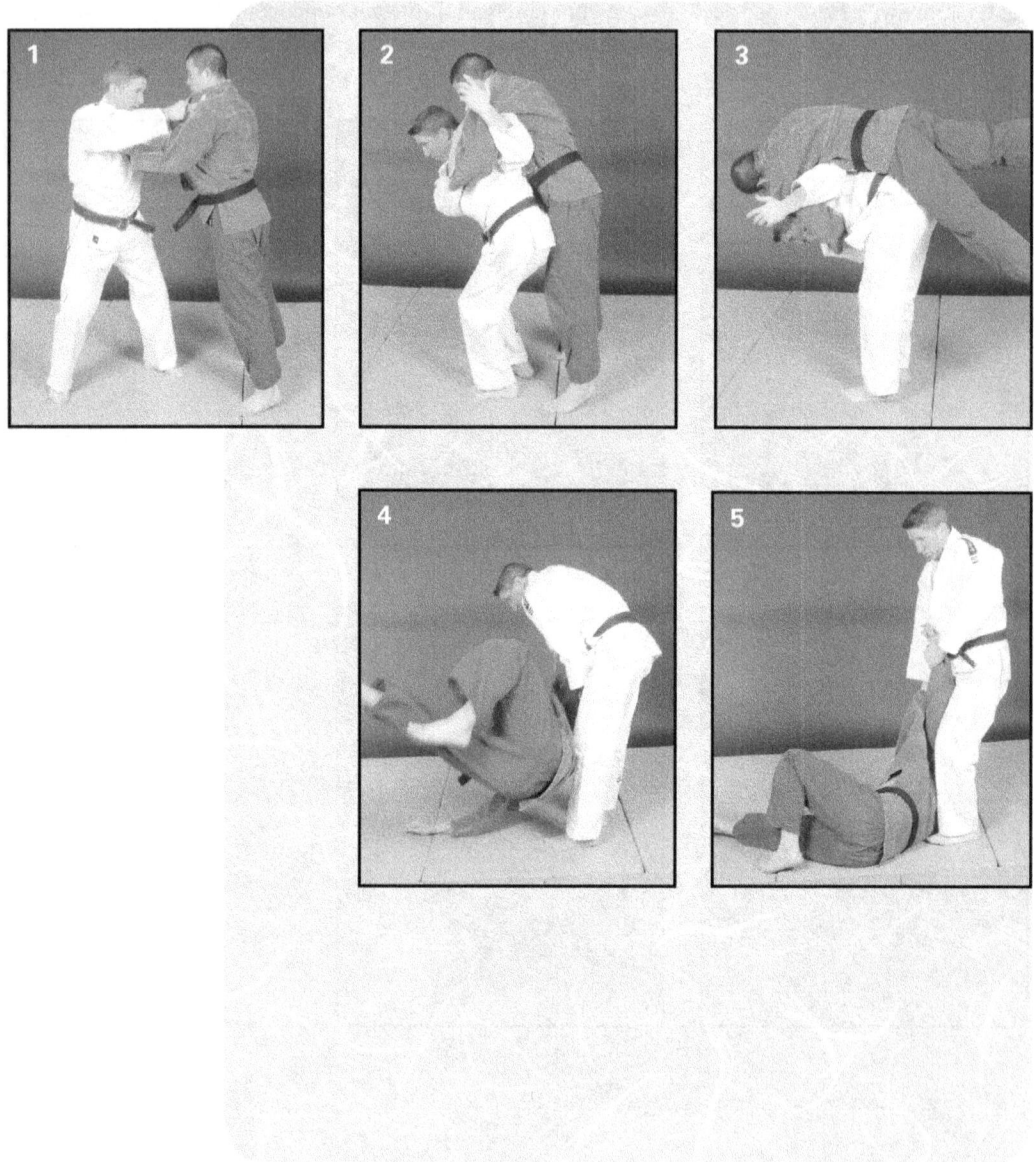

Throwing Techniques

Tai O Toshi Basic (Side Body Drop)

The most important key to this hand throw is the direction of the throw. Off-balance and throw your opponent to her forward corner. In comparison, this direction is different from Seio Nage, which is straight forward. Forward off-balancing is done by both hands/wrists with the sleeve hand pulling straight out first, then down during the follow through. It is critical to leave a little space between you and your opponent. Use this space to pull your opponent over your lower leg. Try not to spread your legs too wide after the pivot. Drop your shoulder on the side of your body your opponent is going over. Your lapel hand should be under your opponent's ear, guiding her as you throw.

Championship Judo

Tai O Toshi Variation #1 (Left Against Right)

The key to this throw is getting your body (shoulder) past your opponent's defense (see close up #1 on page 14). Take a big step sideways and push the back of your wrist into your opponent's wrist. Your pulling arm, which grabs the sleeve, should pull out and then down, keeping your pinkie finger up. Make sure you throw in a diagonal direction off the side of your body.

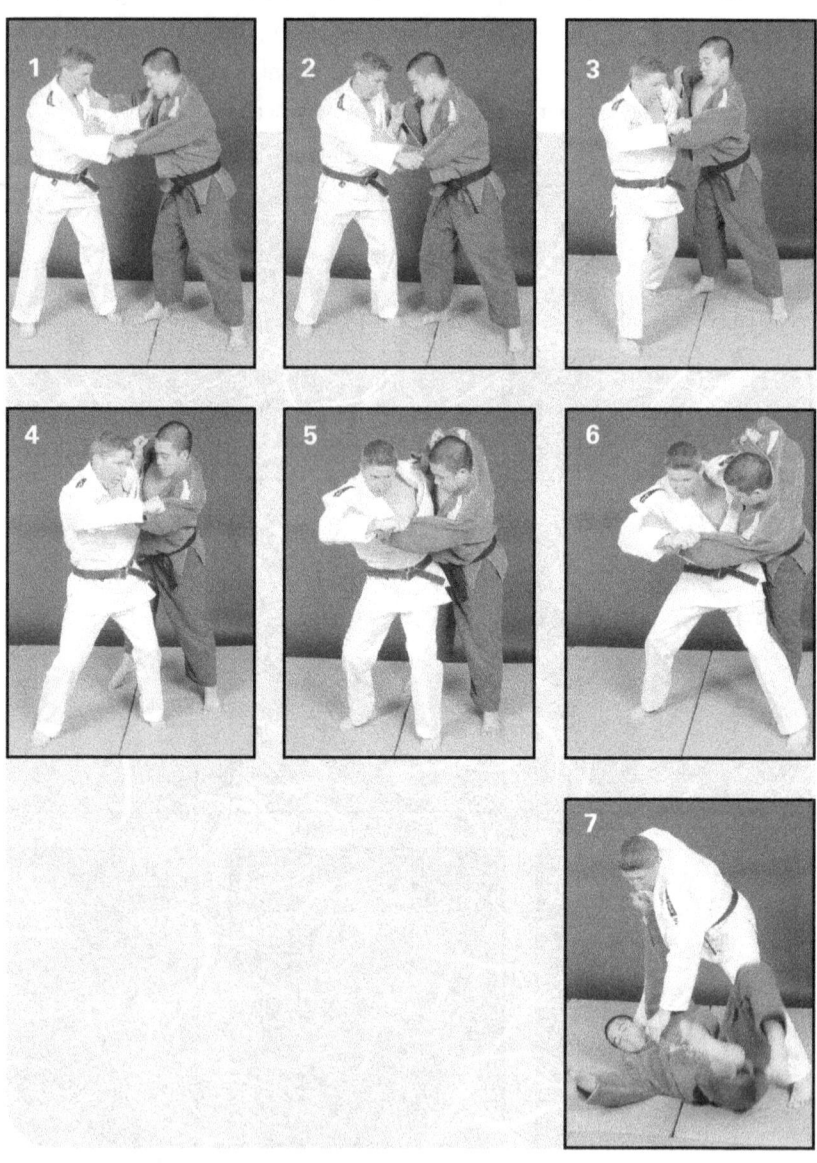

Throwing Techniques

Ouchi Gari Basic (Big Inner Reap)

This leg technique is one that I personally used effectively in competition many times throughout my career. The best time to attack is when the opponent is pulling or leaning on his heels. The critical point is to attack with your whole body, after using your wrists to snap forward as you enter. By snapping your opponent forward, it causes your opponent to react by pulling back, giving you the precise time to get into position and follow through. Also, this is a great technique to set up a forward throw because your opponent pushes back to stop this throw, which opens him up for a forward throw.

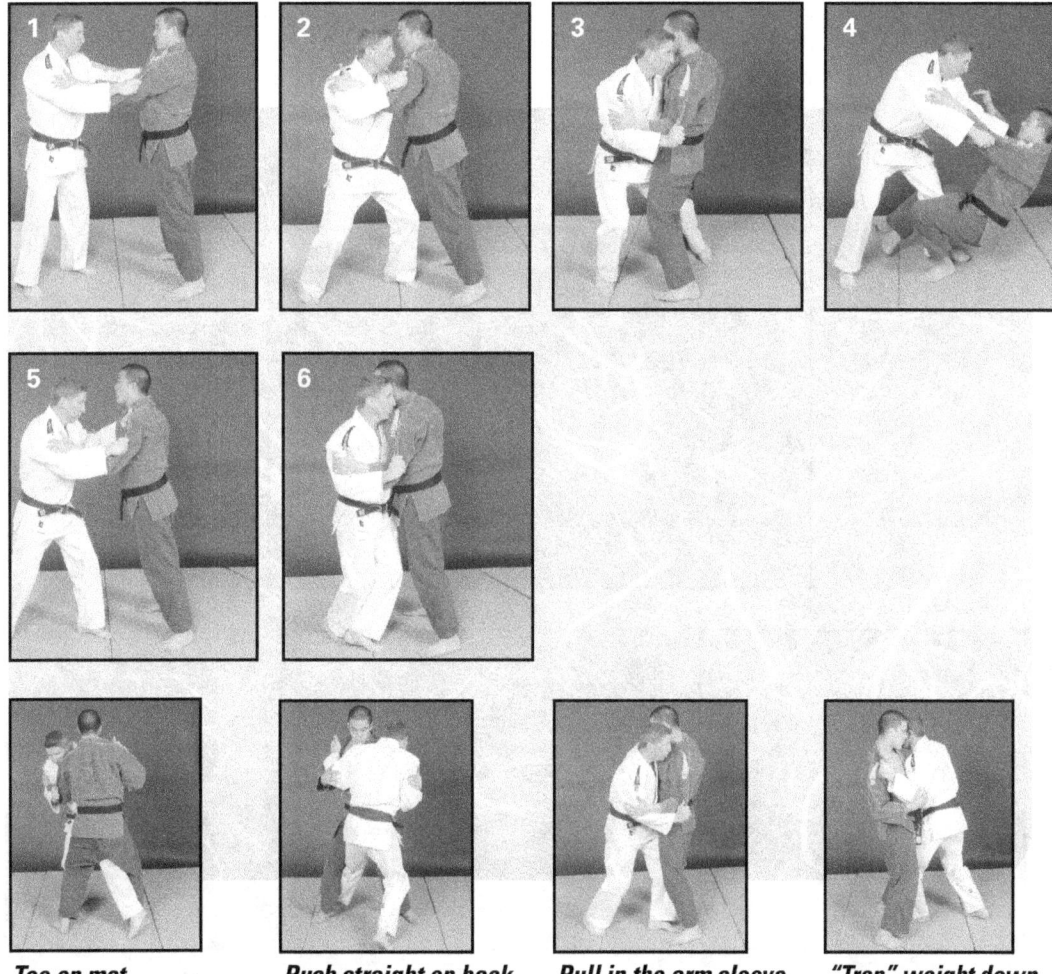

| Toe on mat | Push straight on back | Pull in the arm sleeve | "Trap" weight down |

Championship Judo

Ouchi Gari Variation #1 (From Lapel Twist)

Start by standing opposite of your normal stance. If I am a lefty then I take a right stance with my right foot forward, gripping my opponent's left lapel with my right hand. Swing yourself into your opponent and trap her side with your arm around her waist. Keep your hand on the same side of your lapel pulling. Be sure to stay low and push straight back from your opponent with your whole body.

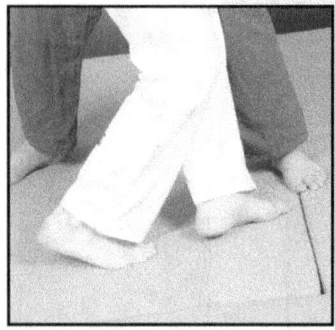

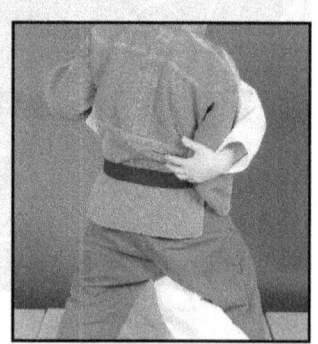

Detail #2 *Detail #3* *Left-hand trap*

Throwing Techniques

Ouchi Gari Variation #2 (Left Against Right—Lower Core Reap)

This move is similar to the initial set up for Tai o Toshi. As your opponent defends and pulls back, reverse your direction and attack to the rear by holding your opponent's leg. To keep from being countered, it is critical to control the sleeve hand and finish the throw.

Championship Judo

De Ashi Barai Basic (Foot Sweep)

Foot sweeps are the essence of real judo because it takes pure timing and technique to throw your opponent. De Ashi means "advanced foot." This is the foot you should attack/sweep as your opponent steps forward or backwards. The time to sweep is when the weight of the foot is almost on the mat or almost off the mat. The key to foot sweeps is setting up your opponent to make your opponent step forward or backwards. It's critical to never cross your feet; as you move around, always try to keep your feet shoulder width apart.

Throwing Techniques

De Ashi Barai Variation #1 (Circle Sweep)

Move your opponent in a small circle counterclockwise. As your opponent follows your lead, sweep one foot into the other. This move takes little strength, but a very high degree of technique and timing. No matter the size of your opponent, this technique can work quite effectively. It is important to use your hands and upper body like a steering wheel to guide your opponent.

  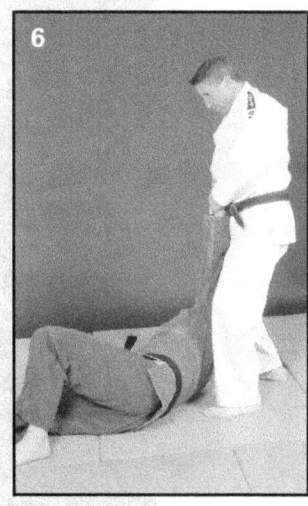

Ippon Seio Counter #1 (Wrist Post)

Controlling the sleeve is extremely important, especially when defending against seio nage (shoulder throw). Simply turn your wrist out and down with the pinkie finger up. Also, keep your feet/body moving so your opponent cannot set up again. Bend your knees and let your opponent feel all of your weight by relaxing and lowering your core body.

Throwing Techniques

Ippon Seio Counter #2 (Hip Lift)

In this counter, side step the attack and lower your core. Keep your back straight and your knees bent. Use your hips to lift your opponent off-balance or just drive your opponent to the side and over. You must first block the attack with a hip check to stop her momentum, and then you can continue to lift and throw.

Championship Judo

Tai O Toshi Counter (Foot Trap)

It is important from the start to have straight posture. As your opponent attacks, block first with a hip check, then slide to the side and hook your opponent's ankle with your instep, pulling it out sideways and straight up. Finish this counter by extending your leg up and rotating your body inwards.

Throwing Techniques

Ouchi Gari Counter—Sasai (Leg Sweep Left to Left)

As your opponent attacks with an inner sweep, pivot sideways, keeping your weight off your sweeping foot. Turn the sweeping foot in and keep your leg straight while the supporting leg stays slightly bent. Use your upper body/hands to rotate your opponent until he falls.

Ouchi Gari Counter—Hiza (Knee Sweep Right to Left)

This counter is much easier to feel than Sasai, because the opponent attacks your advanced foot. The key is to keep your lapel hand elbow down, posting weight on your opponent's attacking leg. Pivot quickly and rotate your opponent. In this counter, I drop the knee (Hiza) instead of the ankle.

Throwing Techniques

De Ashi Barai Counter—De Ashi Barai (Foot Sweep)

This counter is all about timing. As your opponent attacks your advanced foot, pull your head back and up, and then sweep your opponent's attacking foot. It is important to pull down on the sleeve or lapel to finish the throw. Make sure you do not lift your knee, only your foot, on the counter to execute a quick and effective counter.

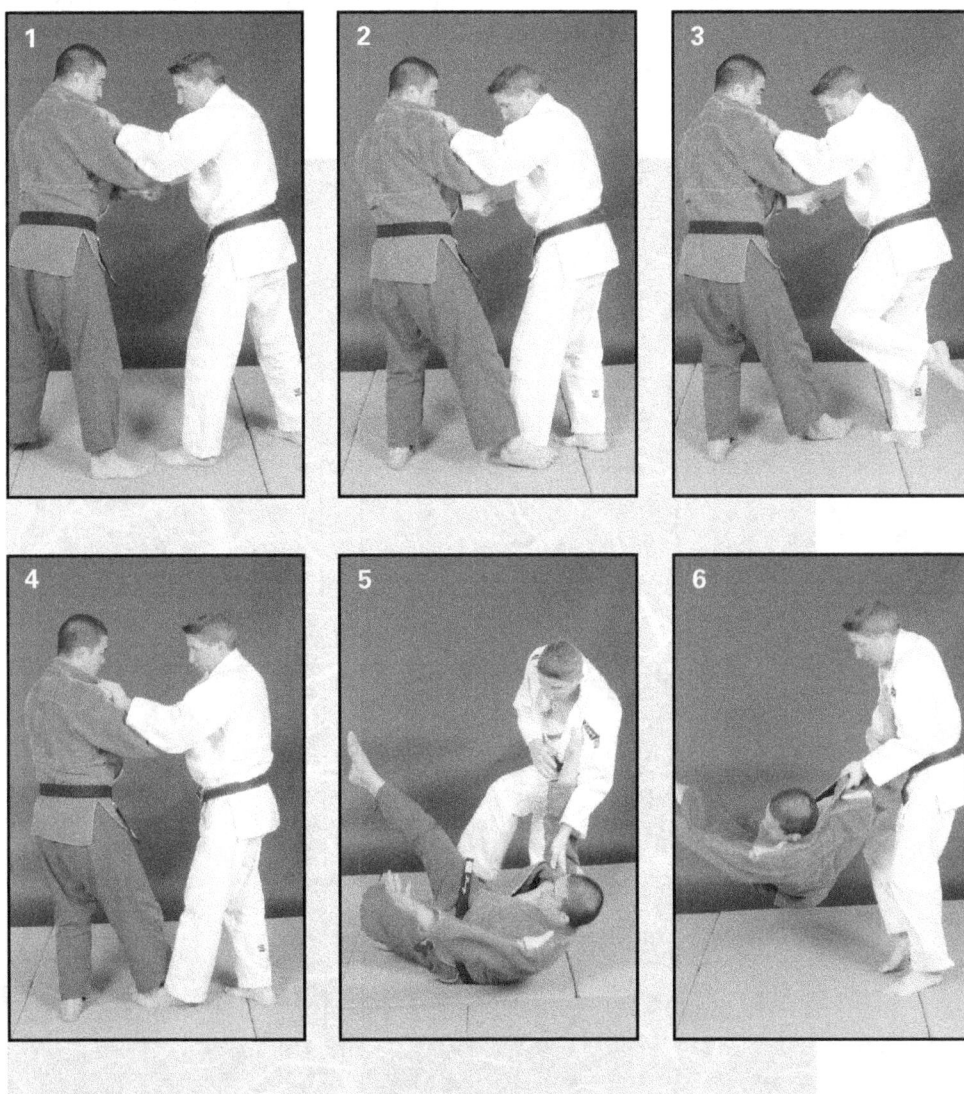

Throwing Combinations

Ouchi Gari to Tai O Toshi

In judo it is extremely important to have an effective rear and forward throw, so that your opponent will be confused as to which direction you will finish the throw. In this combination, attack to the rear first with an inner sweep (ouchi gari) to make your opponent push back. It is critical to take advantage of this reaction and pull/snap your opponent forward with both hands before attacking forward.

Throwing Techniques

Ouchi Gari to Tai O Toshi (different view)

Here is a different view of ouchi gari to tai o toshi. Notice how the pulling arm off-balances your opponent before you pivot into position.

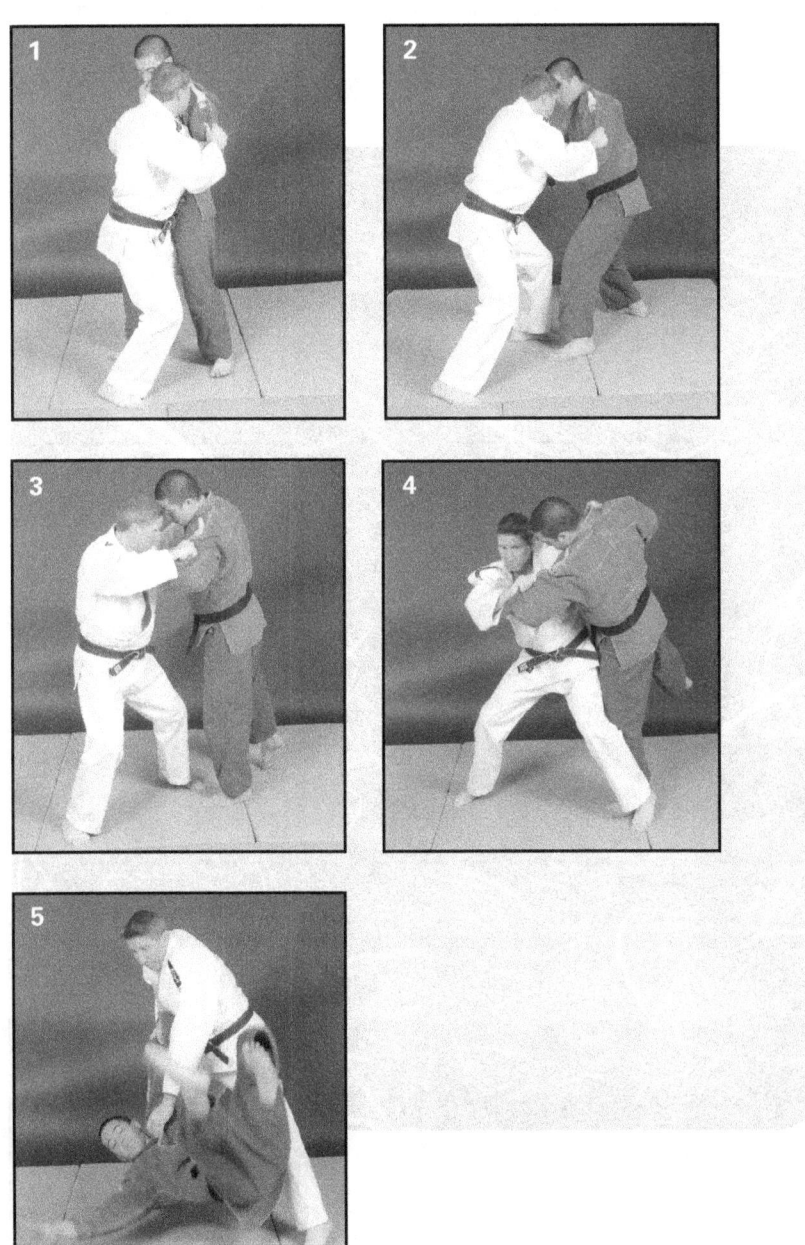

Ouchi Gari to Ippon Seio

The key to this shoulder throw combo is to make a very tight position, locking in your opponent's arm. The sleeve hand locks down on the ouchi gari attack, but then pulls up and across your chest on the ippon seio throw.

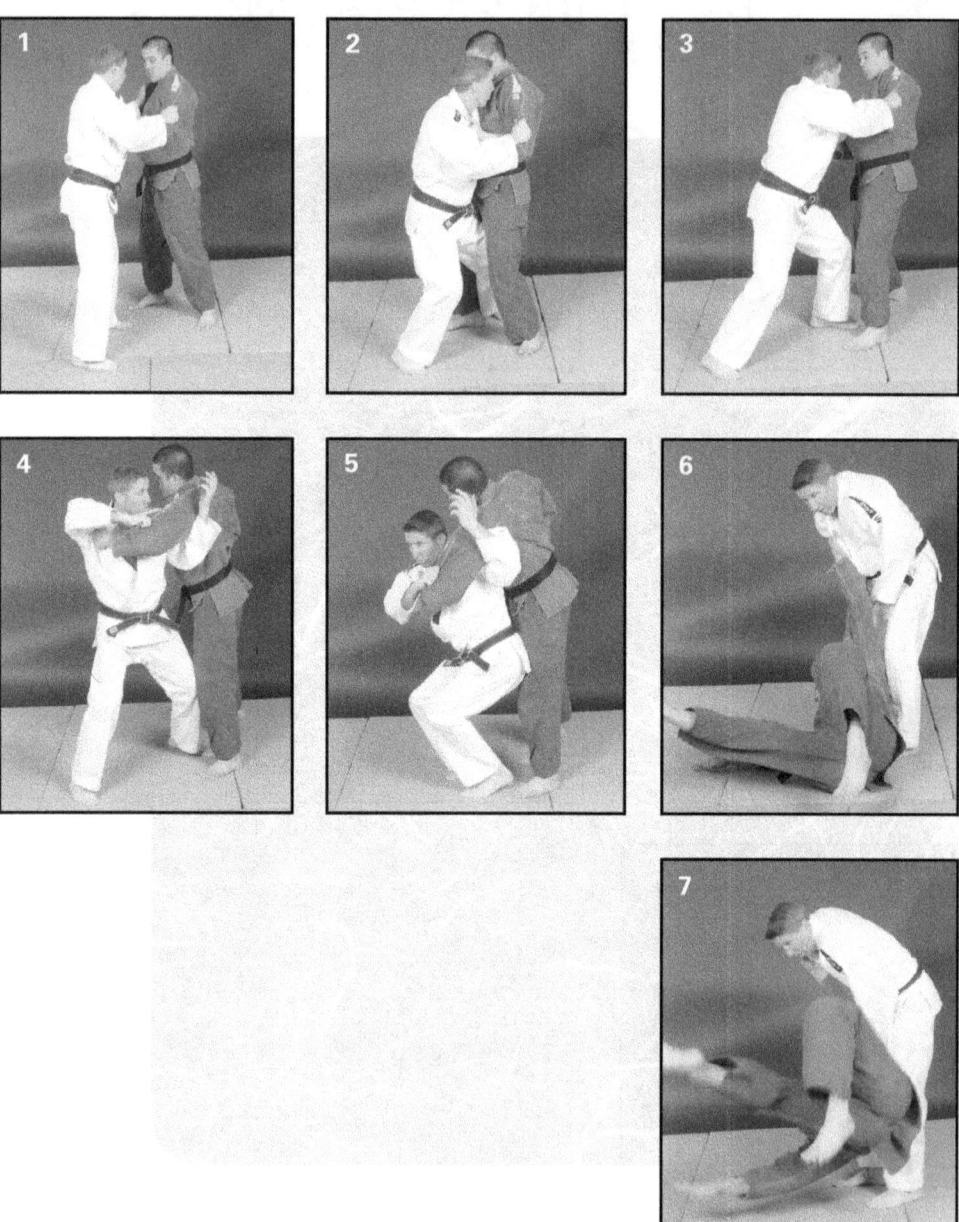

Throwing Techniques

Ouchi Gari to De Ashi Barai

In order to execute this technique you must have movement. After attacking ouchi gari, as your opponent steps back, use your wrists to snap her upper body forward while sweeping his leg.

Championship Judo

Sasae Tsurikomi Ashi (ankle sweep)

Start with a standard grip (1). Pull your opponent's left leg forward (2), propping your foot against his ankle and pulling up and out on their leading arm (3). Then, rotate your upper body as if you were turning a big wheel (4), and finish (5).

Throwing Techniques

Uchi Mata (inner thigh throw)

From a standard left side high collar grip (1), pull your opponent onto his toes in order to bring him off balance (2). Turn your hips and head continuing to pull forward (3). Your left leg should maneuver up in between opponent's legs (4), and finish by holding opponents arm to help break the fall (5).

Uki Goshi (quarter hip throw)

Start with a standard grip (1). Step in with your left foot while pulling your opponent towards you (2). Lift the opponent on to the side of your hip (3), and finish with the throw (4).

Throwing Techniques

Harai Goshi variation (big step sweeping leg throw)

Start with a standard grip (1). Pull opponent forward on his toes and step in front of opponent's right foot (2). Pivot strong on your right foot stepping across opponent's body with left leg (3). Continue to pull forward and rotate your body (4), to apply the throw (5).

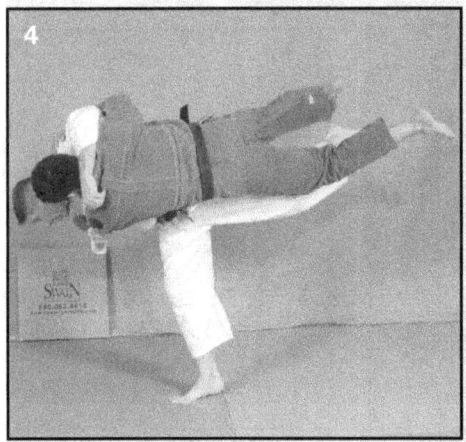 

Koshi Guruma (head and arm throw)

From a standard grip (1), pull opponent into you while stepping to the top of the triangle (2). Pull opponent's head forward keeping him off balance, bend your knees, keep your back straight and keep your feet a shoulder width apart (3). Then, rotate your body while maintaining balance (4), and finish the throw (5).

Throwing Techniques

Kouchi Gari (inside leg trip)

From standard grip (1), pull your opponent forward while stepping in at the same time (2). Keep the opponent tight to your body while trapping opponent's foot with the sole of your foot (3). Then, throw straight back pushing off your right foot and sweeping with your left (4). The key to this throw is the direction you throw the opponent – straight back and not to the side.

Kosoto Gari (outside ankle trip)

In this case the opponent has a high grip and you have the inside grip (1). As opponent steps forward with his right foot, trap or post the ankle with your left foot (2) Sweep the foot while pushing opponent backwards (3), and finish the throw with control (4). The key is in step #3, controlling opponent's left sleeve by pushing down so he cannot counter.

Throwing Techniques

Tani Otoshi (back drop)

Opponent has an offensive grip and stance (1). When the opponent attacks with a forward hip throw, block with your left hip (2), slide your leg behind both legs of the opponent while controlling their upper body (3), and take opponent backwards for the throw (4). Then, control the mat position (5). The key is to block first with your hips before trying to counter with the backdrop.

Championship Judo

Sukui Nage (back sacrifice)

Starting form a right to left stance (1), pull your opponent in with two grips on one sleeve (2). As opponent reaches out with his left hand to escape and pull, take a wide stance and step behind him while reaching in front with your left arm (3). Then, turn into your opponent while springing backwards (4), and finish with side control (5).

 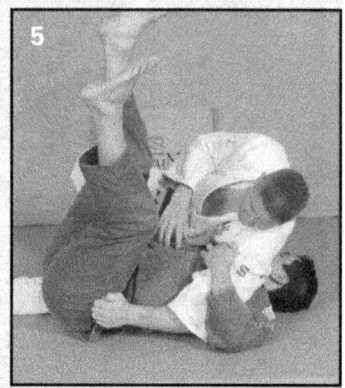

Throwing Techniques

Morote Seio Nage (sleeve wrap hip throw)

Starting form a standard lapel and sleeve grip (1), pull the opponent forward while stepping in (2). Wrap his lapel in your left hand while bending your arm and placing your elbow into his armpit (3), bend your knees, keeping your back straight up (4). Spring forward on to your toes extending your knees (5), to finish the throw (6).

Kata Garuma Variation (shoulder wheel)

From a standard grip (1), pull the opponent's left arm over your shoulder while stepping between his legs in a squat balanced position (2). Then, bring your right foot back to your left while springing up to the left side of your opponent, rotating forward (3), to finish the throw (4).

Throwing Techniques

Leg Pick To Ouchi Gari

From an extreme right to left stance (1), trap opponent's arm under your chin lowering your core and leaning in (2). Then, pick the ankle up at the right moment (3), sweep out the rear leg while keeping your toes on the mat and making a semi circle (4). Then finish with a strong rotation (5),

Morote Gari (double leg scoop)

Before gripping starts, bring your body low (1), change levels and slide in putting your hands behind opponent's knees (2). Scoop up his legs while standing up (3), and finish strong until opponent lands flat on his back (4).

Throwing Techniques

Soto Maki Komi (trapping leg throw)

Start from a standard grip (1). Pull opponent forward and reach over his shoulder (2). Lock your body into your opponent's and continue to pull with your body (3). Then, finish by falling with your opponent for maximum torque (4).

Ushiro Goshi (back throw)

From a right hand lapel grip (1), block your opponent's attack with your hip (2), and lift the opponent as he exits the throw (3). Then, force him straight back (4), and finish with side control (5).

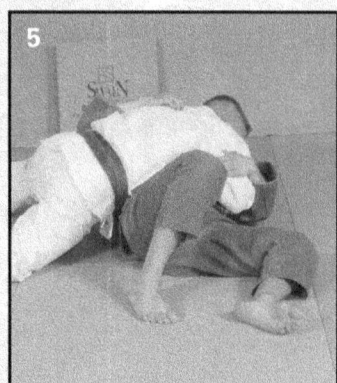

Throwing Techniques

Utsuri Goshi (changing hip throw)

From a right to left stance (1), block opponent's attack with hip check (2). Lift opponent with knees not your back (3) and at the peak of the lift, change your hip stance into a basic hip throw (4). Then, follow through with ogoshi (hip throw) (5). Maintain side control in case you need to execute a pin (6).

Sode Tsurikomi Goshi (sleeve throw)

From a standard grip (1), drive the sleeve of the opponent's left arm straight up sticking your elbow into his armpit (2). Then, bring left foot back, pulling the opponent forward and turning into the throw (3). Rotate your body for a right side throw (4), and apply the throw from the proper position (5).

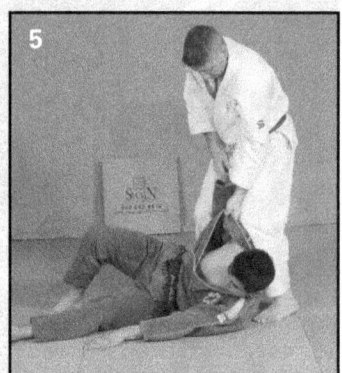

Throwing Techniques

Osoto Guruma (double leg trip)

From a standard grip (1), attack osoto gari snapping the opponent to you while stepping next to his foot (2). Crossover both legs (3), close up (4), and finish strong by taking the opponent straight onto the ground (5). Maintain side control (6).

Harai Goshi (basic sweeping leg throw)

Start in standard stance (1). Pull the opponent forward keeping pivot foot at the top of the triangle with the opponent's feet (2). Then, sweep your leg across opponent's leg while pulling him forward and rotating your body (3). Finish with a throw using all of your body (4).

Throwing Techniques

Ura Nage (back sacrifice throw)

From a right against left stance (1), block opponent's attack with your hip. Bending your knees, lift opponent (2) and fall back while lifting your opponent in a circular motion (3). Front View (4).

Front View

Chapter 3

Judo Grappling

Introduction

There are four ways to win in judo: throwing, pinning, choking and arm locks. Three of these are achieved by grappling. Therefore, it is important for the student to have a strong base in grappling in order to build his/her confidence in executing standing techniques.

Basic Grappling Movements

Before learning the techniques of grappling it is important to first understand the basic movements, theories and drills that relate to all the techniques. Once we learn these fundamentals the correct way, it is much easier to learn the actual technique.

#1: BEACH BALL THEORY

In theory, when you jump on top of a beach ball, you roll off. Therefore, in this position, you can better defend yourself against your attacker. The idea is to stay tucked in a ball while moving in different directions. The key points to remember are to keep your elbows and your knees close together, your head should be off the mat, and your chin tucked in. Try not to stay on your back; try to stay on one side or the other. By staying on your side, you keep your opponent off balance. By defending with your legs and your hands, and staying tucked in a beach ball position, you can easily roll your opponent off of you as he/she attacks.

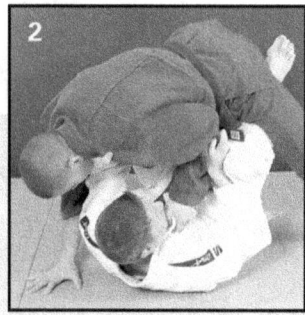
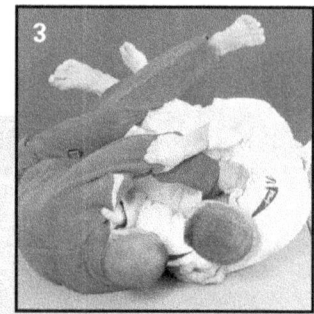

Judo Grappling

Beach ball exercise

Have the students sit in a circle on the mat. Instruct them to hug their knees to their chests and first rock backwards and forwards and then roll backwards all the way down the mat and up again. Have them roll backwards and forwards with their knees tucked into their chests several times. Alternate the rocking motion from backwards and forwards to side to side for several more counts. Begin with the right. Roll down, count 1, straight up, then down left, and up. From this motion, instruct students to roll down and around in a complete circle. If they have difficulty understanding this motion, explain to them that they should act just like they were a beach ball. Keeping their legs tucked into their chests like a beach ball, they roll down and around clockwise from left to right.

#2: HOW TO KEEP YOUR ATTACKER IN FRONT OF YOU

If you let your partner past your legs, then half your defense is gone. This is a critical moment in grappling, and you must prevent this from happening. As in standing judo, the goal is to use your opponent's strength against himself and keep him off balance. By using your legs and feet as hooks on his legs, you make your partner pull you around instead of using your own energy.

There are two basic ways to hook your legs onto your opponent so that he does the work of spinning around.

1) Inside hook
2) Outside hook

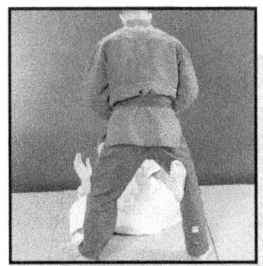
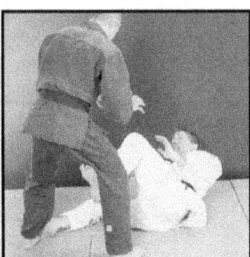
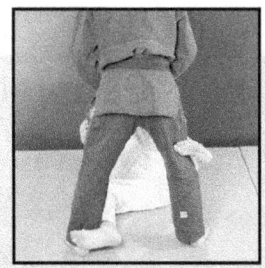

Inside hook   A   B   *Outside hook*   A   B

Championship Judo

#3: REVERSE BICYCLE

This is an important exercise for offense and defense. While lying on your side, keep your hands in front of you, touch your knees to your chest, and fully extend your leg kicking with your heels. Move side to side as you progress with speed.

 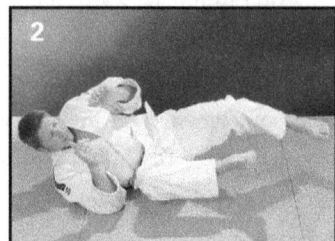 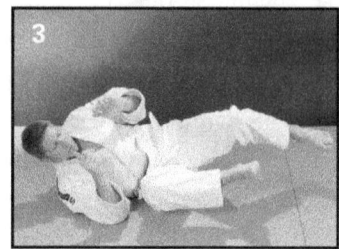

#4: WINDMILL EXERCISE

This drill is important for defense. Start by pointing the toes in the air and drawing two circles in the opposite directions. Increase your speed by keeping your hips flexible and moving side to side. In a practical application, your feet can be used as two more hands by blocking and hooking your opponent's arms, hips, and legs.

   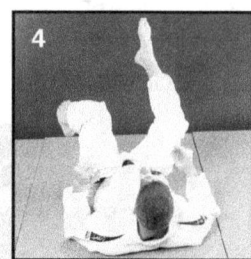

#5: MAT PULLS

This is an essential exercise in learning how to pin. The key points are to keep your head up and look straightforward. Pull your body forward using your arms bent at the elbows at 90° angles. If you pull too far, your hips pop up and you can be easily turned over. Keep your hips down and your legs spread apart while digging your toes into the mat.

  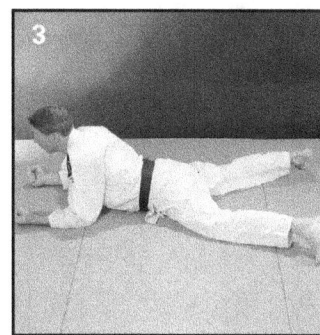

VARIATION TO #5: MAT PULL AND SWITCH

In this exercise, you add a variation of switching from hip to hip. Keep your head straight making sure you do not turn it, otherwise your opponent can turn you over. Keep your hips down on the mat and begin by sliding your bottom leg all the way through.

Championship Judo

#6: SHRIMP CURL EXERCISE

This drill is key to learning how to escape and defend in grappling. Begin by lying on your back. Move your body across the mat while curling like a shrimp. Keep your hips off the mat by digging in with your heels. Keep your elbows close to your body while pushing straight over your head.

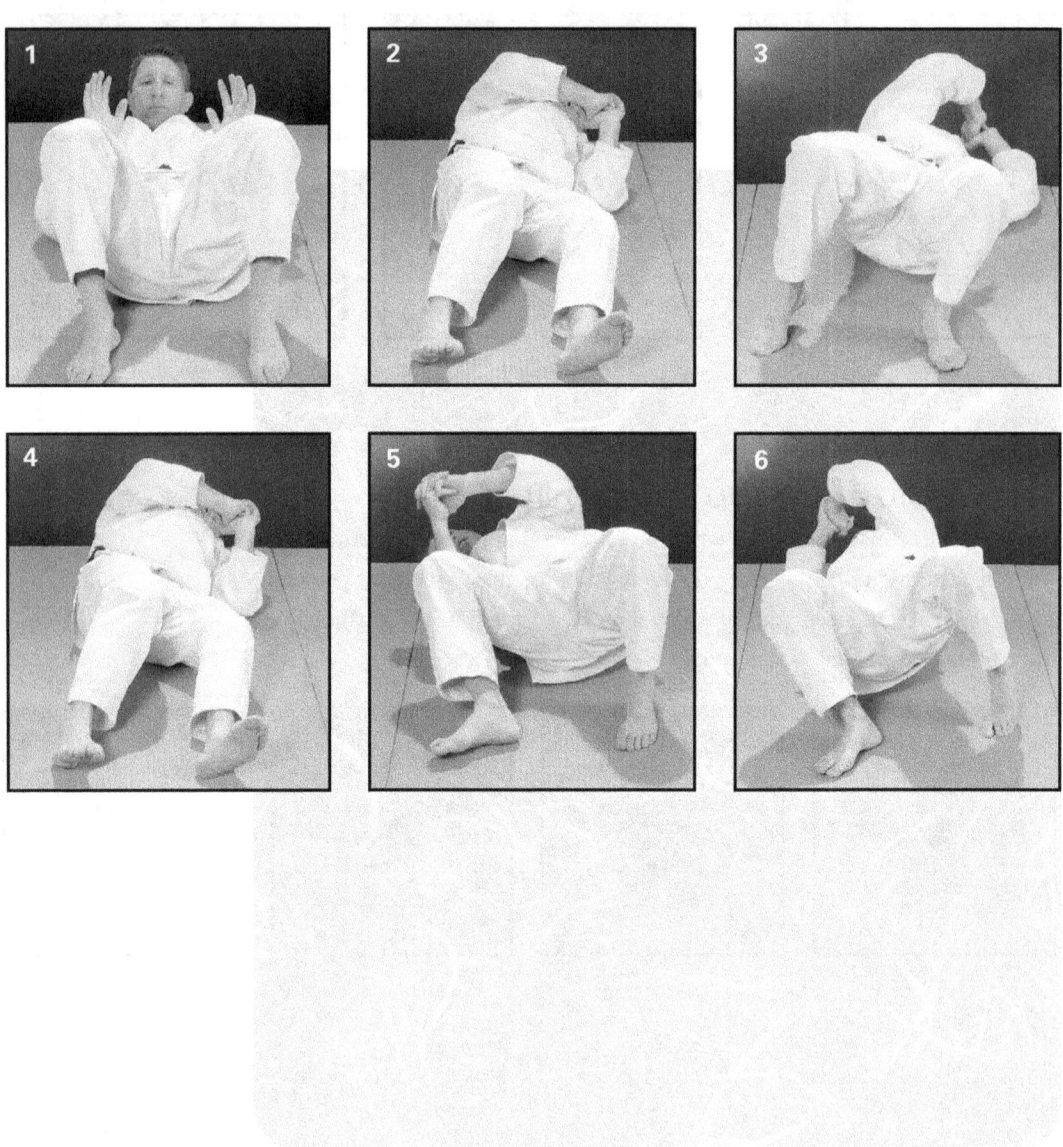

VARIATION TO #6: REVERSE SHRIMP CURL EXERCISE

This is the same drill but the movement is backwards. Keep your hips up, elbows in, and pretend you're pushing your opponent away from you while curling your body into a shrimp. Always keep your head off the mat and your chin tucked in.

Gripping Applications

Bottom Position

The first thing you must do as your opponent is moving closer to you is to sit up to one side and defend yourself using your arms and legs. It's a good idea to grab your opponent first and gain control of the grip before your opponent gains control of you. It is important to control your opponent's head if possible by grabbing high on the inside lapel with a cross grip. If you control the head then the body will follow. The other hand should try to control the lower sleeve. Use the grip to your advantage in offense or defense but do not rely completely on it for both, however do rely on total body movement. Your hips must remain flexible and ready to move in order to keep your attacker off balance. Use your feet to block your opponent's movement and keep your opponent off balance.

Judo Grappling

Top Position

Try to keep your base strong. Keep your head up and hands in front. When approaching your opponent to pass his legs, grab the pant legs low for control. If possible pull him forward to extend his legs and pass. Work against one leg at a time. Gain control of the leg by squeezing your knees together and keeping your hips low to the mat. Next control your opponent's head and neck. Only then can you try to pull your leg out. Next walk your foot, heel to toe sideways, until your opponent only has hold of your ankle. This loosens his grip making it much easier for you to get your leg out. Point your toe, straighten your leg, and slide your hips all the way up; this action will help you pull out your foot. After you have slid your hip up, make sure to keep your weight, or your hipbone, directly on your opponent's ear. This will keep him flat on his back. Switching your hips will stop him from bridging up and turning you over.

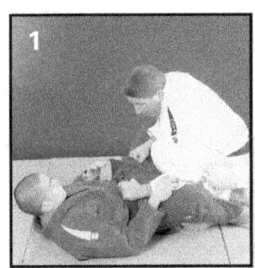

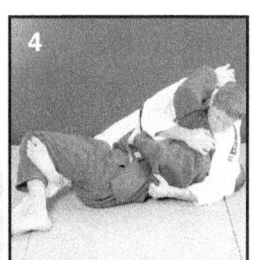

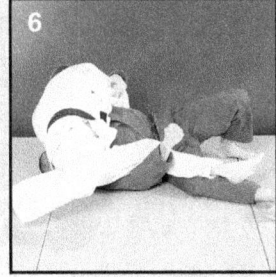
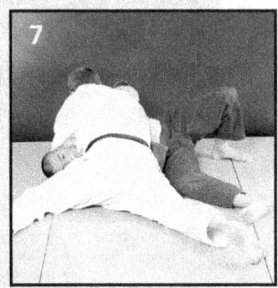

Three (3) Basic Ways to Start a Free-practice in Grappling

1) Back to back—This is a good position for beginners because it forces them to turn and face each other in the proper position.

2) Person #1 on his knees attacking and person #2 on his back defending—It's important for the attacker to maintain his balance by keeping his head up and his stomach forward until he gets past the leg. The very first move taught to beginners is gaining control of the opponent's head and chest. From a kneeling position, break through your opponent's defense, bear hug his chest, and control his head by using your shoulder to apply pressure underneath his chin.

3) Person #1 down on the mat on his elbows and knees and person #2 attacking from behind—This position often occurs in judo following a failed attack or the attacker is blocked bringing him down to the mat. Because this is the worst position to be in, you must quickly turn and face your opponent. Keep your elbows in and your hands up to protect yourself from being choked or arm locked. Then quickly turn and face your opponent. This puts you in a much better position to attack or defend yourself against your opponent.

Basic Gripping and Turnover Methods

Leg Sweep

Cross-grip your opponent's lapel and hold the sleeve just below the elbow. With the bottom of your heel, push his knee out and pull forward on his sleeve. Your other leg stays inside his leg and kicks up to force his body to turn over.

 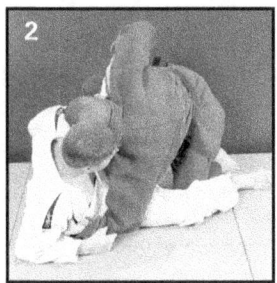 

Side Roll

Beginning in the same position as the leg sweep, cross-grip and grab underneath your opponent's triceps. Next, reach around your opponent's body and grab his belt. Shoot your hips underneath him so that your body is underneath his center of gravity, and roll him to the side coming up on top.

 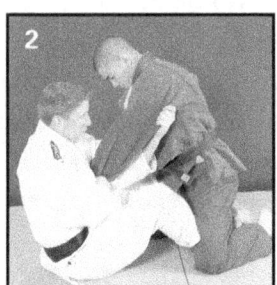 

Controlling the Head Theory

When you apply pressure to the stomach area, your opponent can still sit up. When you apply pressure to his chest, your opponent is still able to move. But when you apply pressure to his head, you control your opponent's body. This theory is very important in pinning and controlling on the ground.

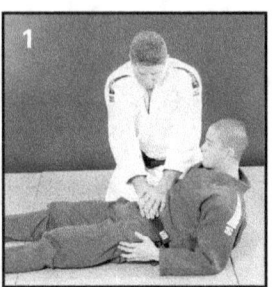 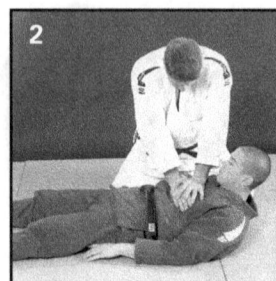 

Osai-komi-waza (Holding Techniques)

Holding Technique #1
Kesa-Gatame (Cross Chest Hold)

The key to pinning is to ensure that you lock your opponent's arm and keep it close to your chest. As you control the arm, ensure that his wrist is locked under your arm. Hold onto the sleeve of the uniform, keep your chest tight, and distribute your weight in a diagonal position. Keep a triangular position, with your head being the top of the triangle, and your two feet being the corners. Use your free hand as a brace so your opponent doesn't roll you over.

Judo Grappling

Variation #1 Makura-Kesa-Gatame (Pillow hold)

The key is to lock the opponent's arm, then wrap around his neck and grab your own knee. Basically your knee becomes a pillow under his neck. Apply pressure by lifting your opponent's head up until you apply the pressure to his chest. This will prevent him from bridging. Keep a triangular position, lock your opponent's head, and hold onto your knee. Grabbing the inside of your leg will apply maximum pressure on your opponent. However, be careful not to get rolled over because your hand is not free to protect you.

Variation #2 Solar plexus

Put your elbow into your opponent's solar plexus. This prevents him from breathing. Apply the pressure directly on his chest. Secure a grip on the uniform's upper half lapel and put his elbow into his chest and lift up. This type is used often in self-defense situations.

Championship Judo

Variation #3 Kuzure-Kesa-Gatame (Under Arm)

Instead of holding your opponent around his neck, place your arm underneath your opponent's arm. The weight distribution is the same. What's important in this variation is that you switch your hips, which enables your body to maintain balance. A key point in this variation is that you are constantly pulling up on your opponent's arm to control his body.

Variation #4 Ushiro-kesa-gatame (Reverse Cross Chest Hold)
Ushiro-Kesa-Gatame (Rear Cross Chest Hold)

Here's a combination from kesa-gatame to ushiro-kesa-gatame. Remember it's very important not to give up the kesa-gatame pin unless you feel like your opponent is escaping. As you feel your opponent escaping, reverse the position and lock the arm. Make sure you hold on to or lock the pants or belt with your free arm or hand. It's important to stay upright. As you're locking the arm, make sure you're grabbing your own belt.

   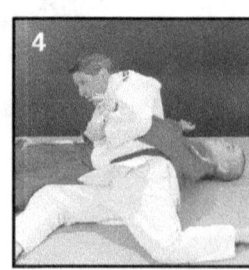

Judo Grappling

Escape from the Kesa-gatame (A)

The key is to try and pull your arm out first, which makes your opponent push back. As he pushes back, grab his belt at the knot and pull in close to your body, put your leg underneath his center of gravity. It's important to switch your hips hard and get your leg underneath. Once you are underneath, bridge up and pull your opponent diagonally over your far shoulder.

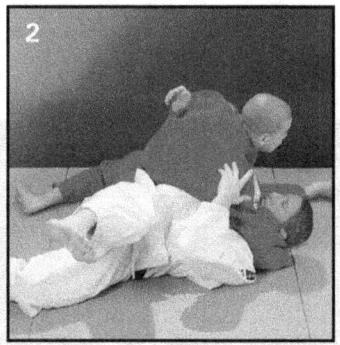

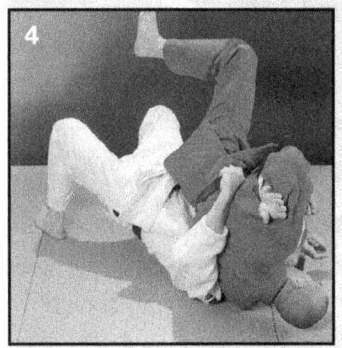
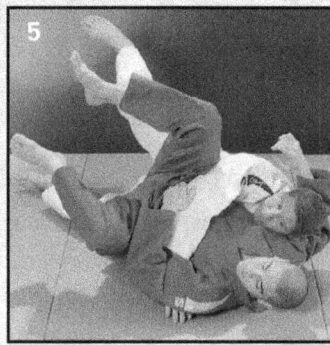

Escape from the Kesa-gatame (B)

This is probably the easiest escape from the pin. Chase your opponent around in a circle and trap his leg by locking it with both of your legs, maintain a scissors-like grip on his legs as you roll him over. Make sure you secure the leg before rolling him over.

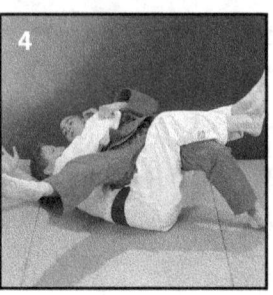 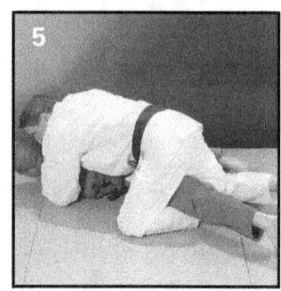

Escape from the Kesa-gatame (C)

The key to this escape is pulling your arm out and driving him forward. Switch your hips to create torque before attempting to pull the arm free, use your free hand to push your opponent forward while pulling your arm out. Get to your knees as soon as possible and follow through by coming on top of your opponent to take control.

 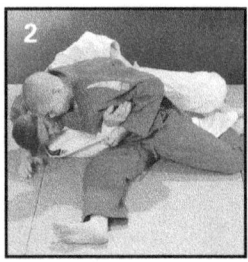  

Judo Grappling

Escape from Kuzure-Kesa Gatame (D)

Reach over your opponent's head and clasp your hands behind the far elbow. Pull both hands toward your head and bridge at the same time. Continue to pull your hands to your far shoulder and bridge through to the top position.

 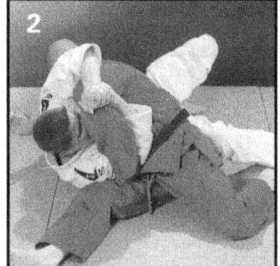 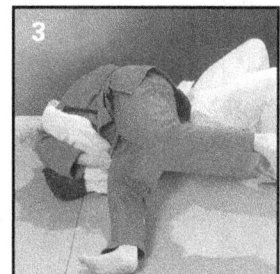

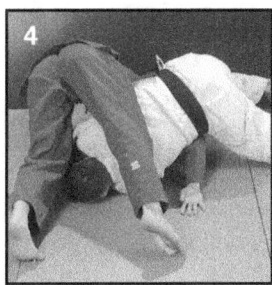 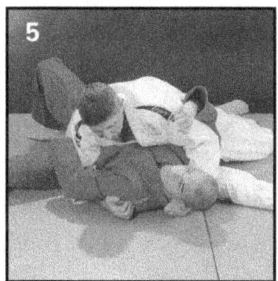

Escape #1 from Ushiro Kesa Gatame (E) (Reverse Kesa Gatame)

It's very important to push and pull the arm out at the same time. This is a very straightforward escape, but it's very important to be explosive. Quickly come on top and control the opponent's body. Again, you're pushing and pulling at the same time. This is very important.

Escape #2 Reverse Kesa Gatame

Try to off balance your opponent forward. When he pushes back, use his momentum and take him back. Hook under the chin to control the head. Switch your hips and legs to come on top.

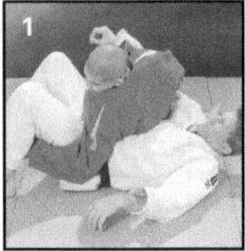  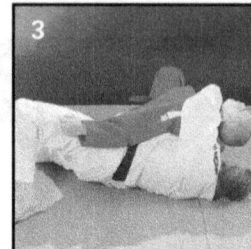 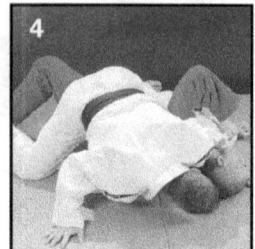

Holding Technique #2
Kami-Shio-Gatame (Shoulder Hold)

It's very important to secure the belt with both hands. Keep it tight and pull it in to yourself. Have your chest put pressure on your opponent's head. Also, keep your hips to the ground. Grab the belt and pull it in to you, as well as keeping your elbows very tight on your opponent. Keep your chin on top of your opponent's chest and push off on your toes into the mat, this will help secure the pin and make it tighter. To make this pin a stronger pin, drop your hips and spread your legs and pull forward. Apply pressure to the head with your chest. As you slip your hips back, make sure you pull on the belt and apply pressure. You may have to move side to side to keep the pressure on top of his chest.

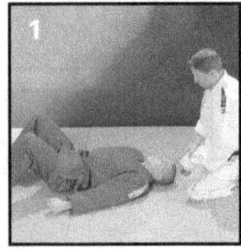  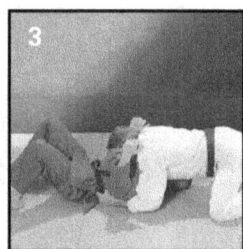 

Judo Grappling

Variation 1

In this variation hold one arm over and one under your opponent's arms. You can slide your hips to the side and apply more pressure on your opponent's head by pulling in to the side of your body. Make sure your elbows are in tight. Slip your hips forward, and continue to keep that triangular position.

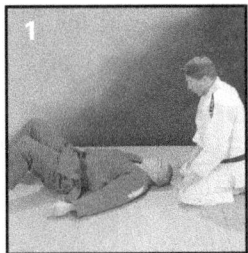 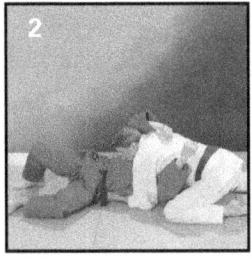 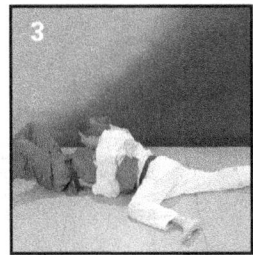 

Note: It's important to grab the belt at the center of the back and use a baseball-type grip to hold your opponent down. Make sure you keep your opponent's head to the side of your ribs and bring your elbows inward. Again it's important to lower your hips, pull forward, and spread your legs. Keep your head up and pull the arms inward.

 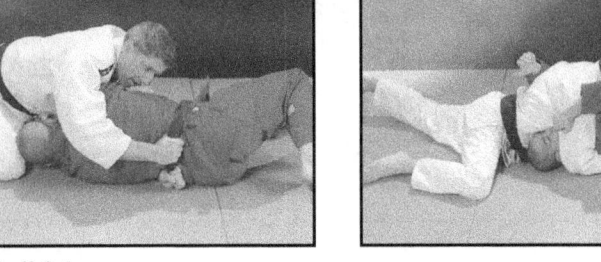

Baseball Grip

Championship Judo

Escape #1 Kami-Shio-Gatame (Shoulder Hold)

First, try to run your opponent in a circle as if you were to gain control of his leg and nullify the pin. As he moves his body around, simply turn him over and put him in the same pin. The idea is to have your opponent straight with your body so he's easier to turn. To help flip him over, grab the inside of his leg with one hand. Use the other hand to grip his belt and pull him over your head. Once he's in a straight line, you simply flip him over. When you go for that initial belt grip, use your whole body to come across his shoulders and grip as deep as you can. You do this by switching your hips.

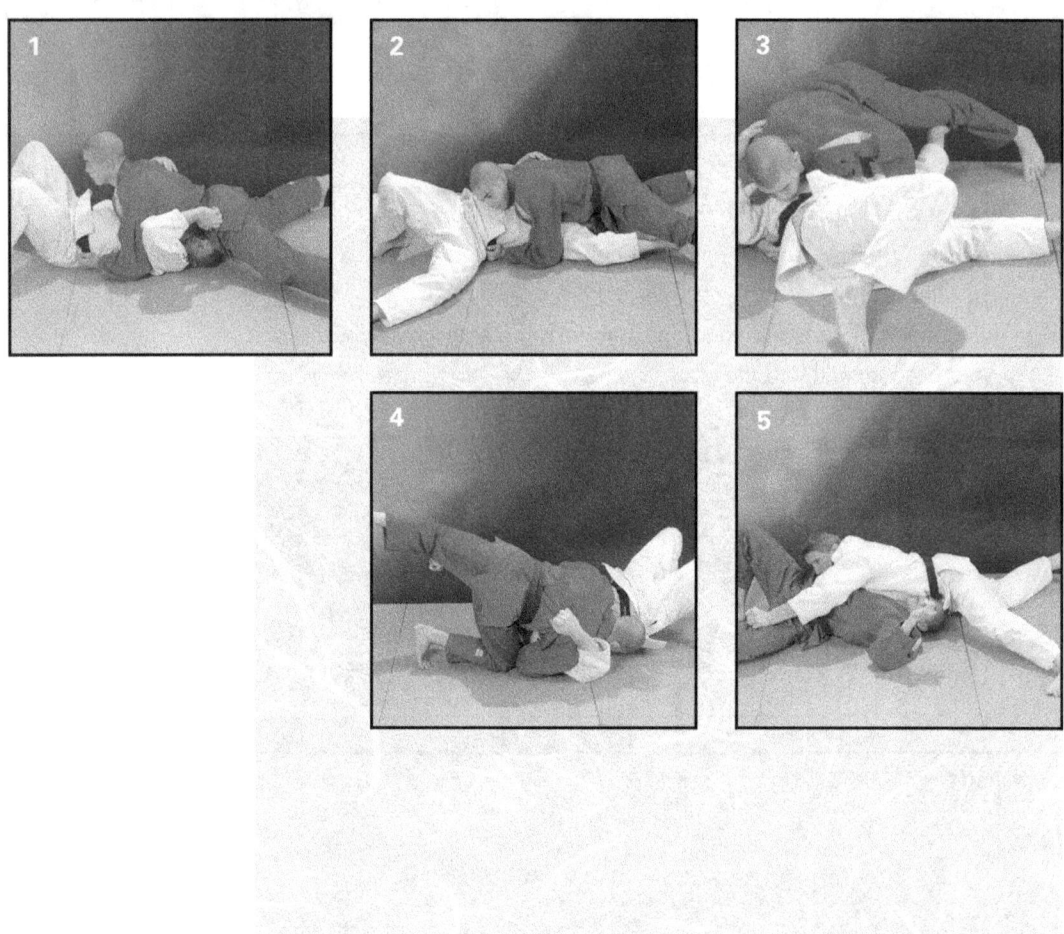

Holding Technique #3
Tate-Shio-Gatame (Four Corners Pin)

Like kimo-shio-gatame, you want to make sure to grab your opponent's belt along the center of his back. Grab his arm up and climb on top of his body and put your heels underneath his hips. Make sure your body is pressed closely to his chest and secure his arms. You can also grab your own lapel to make sure it's tight. Put your head forward and press down on his chest.

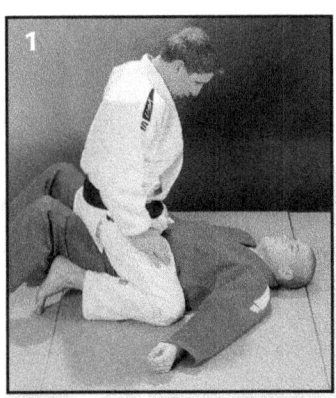
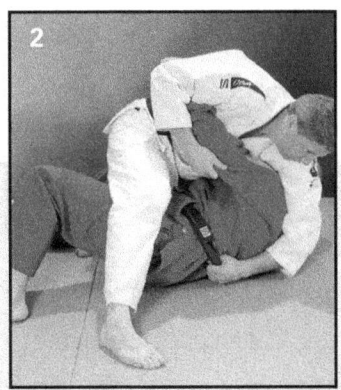

Championship Judo

Variation #1 (Four Corners Pin)

You can modify this pin slightly by bringing your legs up higher on the pin and securing your opponent's shoulders. You want to make sure that you push both of your opponent's arms above his head, lock your arms underneath his head, and squeeze. Make sure your body is tight to his and your hips are down. You must also have your heels tucked tightly under his hips to keep a good, secure balance. To apply pressure you can move forward. You can also use your arm as a brace to stop your opponents bridge.

Judo Grappling

Escape Tate-Shio-Gatame #1

When your opponent has pinned you in tate-shio-gatame, it is important for you to pull your locked arm inward and drive your opponent's head down and body forward. Make sure you trap the outside of his ankle with your foot, then roll on top of him. Push forward and pull in that locked arm.

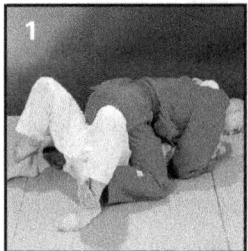 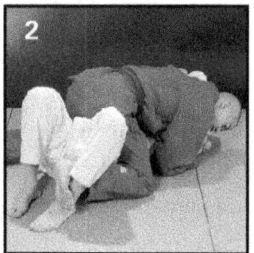 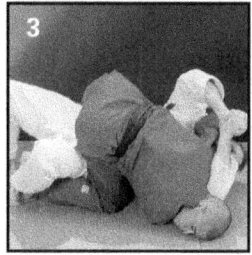 

Escape Tate-Shio-Gatame #2

In this escape it is important to switch your hips to off balance your opponent. Then push your opponent's knee down in between your legs and lock. You can then switch your hips again to the other side to escape and come on top.

  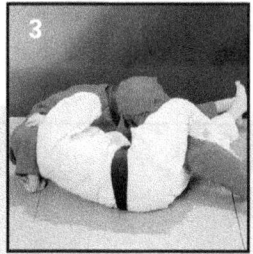 

Pinning Drills

Floating the Pin

Now let's take a look at some of the holds we just learned and put them together with a simple grappling drill called floating the pin. Basically, you want to stay on top your opponent, control his head, switch your hips keeping your hips low to the ground and distribute your weight the correct way. You must control his head. This is the most important part. If you can control your opponent's head, his body will follow. The concept is to be like a sack of rice. You want to relax and be dead weight on top your opponent. Float or glide from pin to pin maintaining the same pressure to keep control. Try not to squeeze too tight but remain relaxed and flexible. This can be used as a 30 sec. drill to warm up. Secure one hold then float to another.

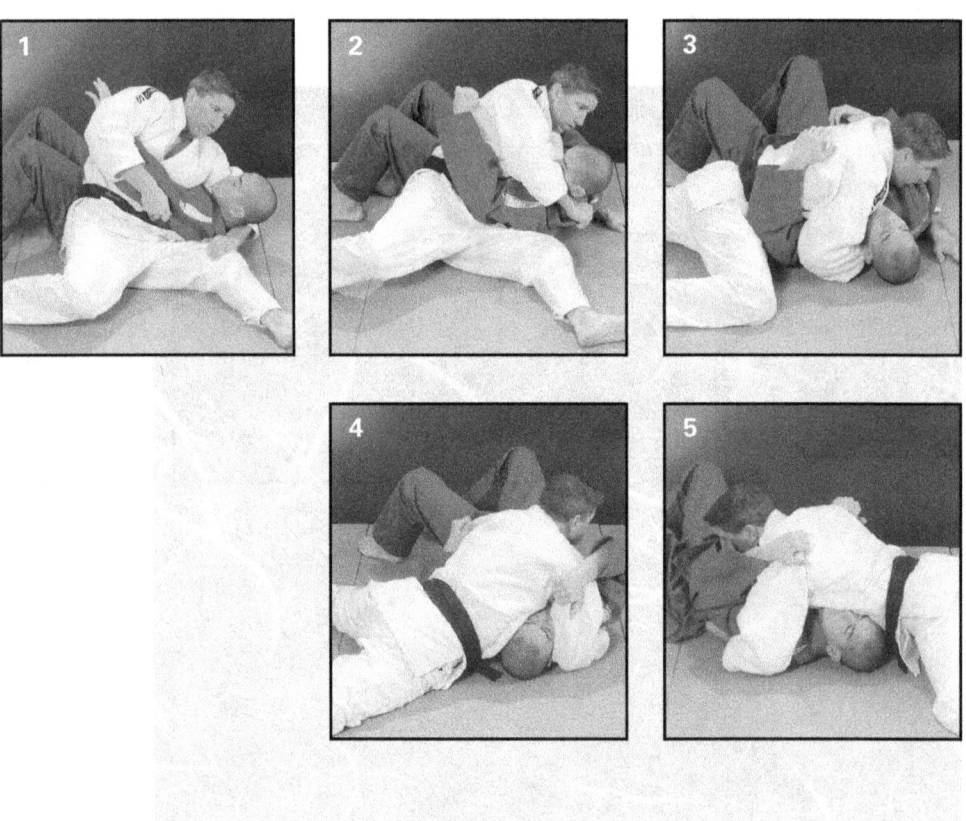

Judo Grappling

Holding Technique #4
Yoko Shio Gatame—Basic (Side Mount)

In this cross mount pin, secure your opponent's upper body with your thumb on the inside of your opponent's collar (see close up 5), pull in and apply pressure with your shoulder to his chin. Your chest should be on top of your opponent's chest, but more importantly, relax your body and become dead weight by exhaling. Control your opponent's lower body by gripping the inside of his pant leg, turning your palm down. Always keep your hips low to the ground. Switch your hips back and forth to keep your opponent from escaping (see close ups #1–#4).

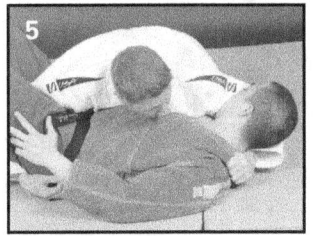

#1

#2

#3

#4

Variant of Legs

115

Championship Judo

Yoko Shio Variation #1

Here is a variation of the yoko shio (cross mount). Control the upper half of your opponent by gripping down the center of her back. It is extremely important to tuck your elbow into your side to control your opponent's head so she cannot bridge.

 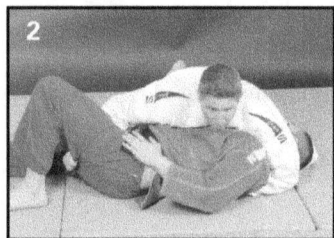 

Holding Technique #5
Kata Gatame—Basic (From the Mount)

In this shoulder lock pin, trap your opponent's head and arm together using pressure from the side of your own head. Extend your leg forward for balance and to stop your opponent from escaping. Keep your other knee bent and close to the body.

Judo Grappling

Kata Gatame (Variation) — Tate Shio Gatame (From the Mount)

From the mount, control the upper half by trapping the head and arm and then jump out to the side for the pin. This position also becomes a choke just by pushing into your opponent with your entire body.

 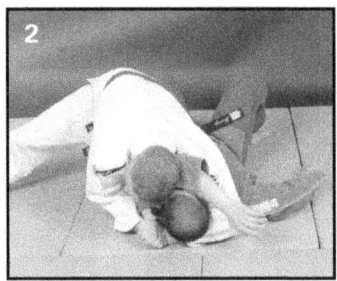 

Escape Yoko Shio #1 (Shrimp — Catch Leg)

In this escape, shrimp out and push your opponent's hip out using your bottom hand. At the same moment, catch the inside leg and lock it up with both your legs in a figure-four to nullify the pin.

Championship Judo

Escape Yoko Shio #2 (Arm Lock Escape)

Escaping yoko shio is done by creating space. Push the side of your opponent's head down and catch the head with your leg. Straighten your opponent's neck hold and catch the elbow joint with your forearm twisting your whole body until your opponent rolls. Come on top and secure the pin.

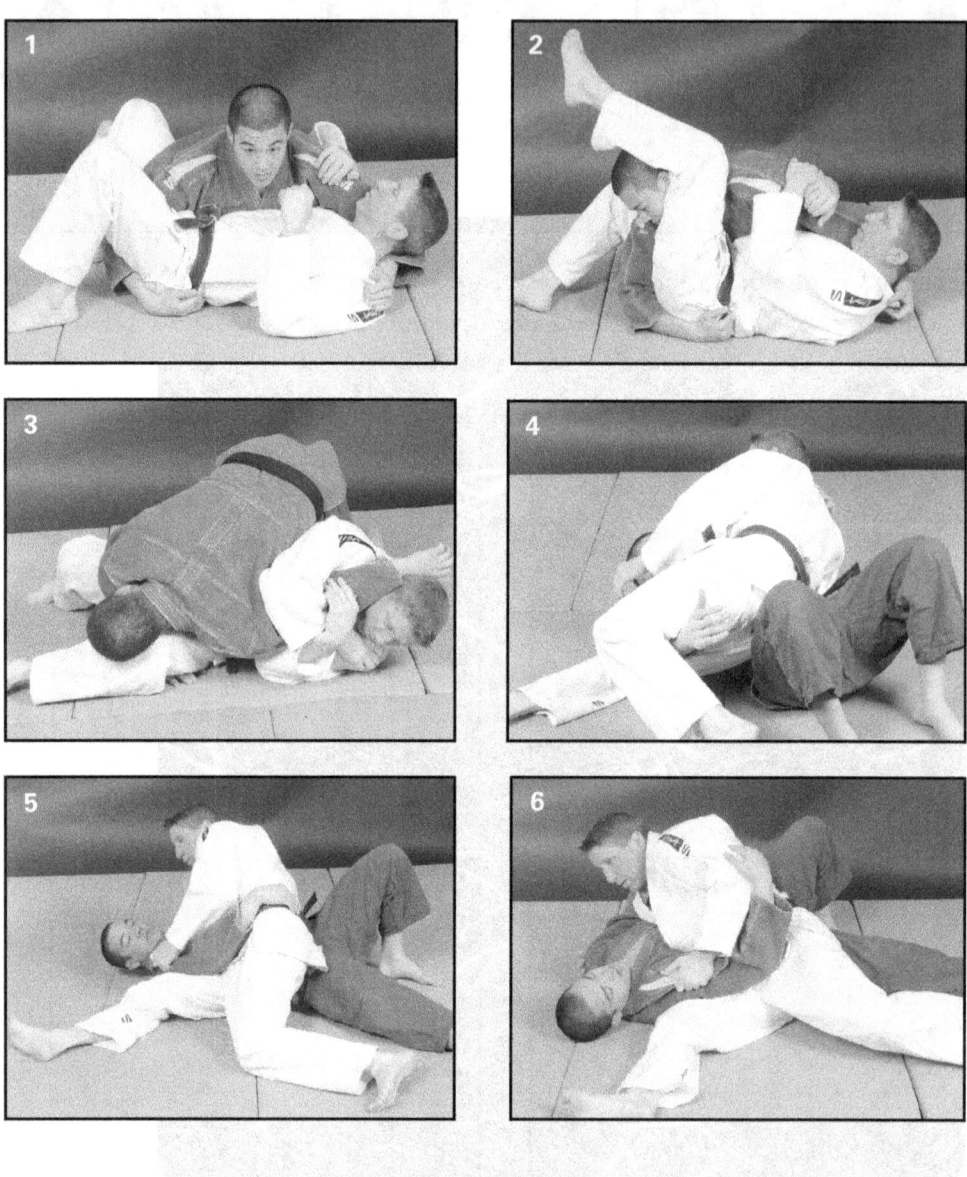

Judo Grappling

Escape Kata Gatame #1

This is a tough pin to escape from because there is a lot of pressure on your arm and head. First, release the pressure and make a small space. Immediately shrimp into your opponent, pushing away on your neck and coming up behind for control.

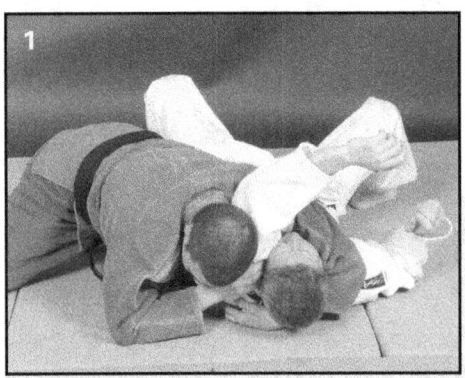
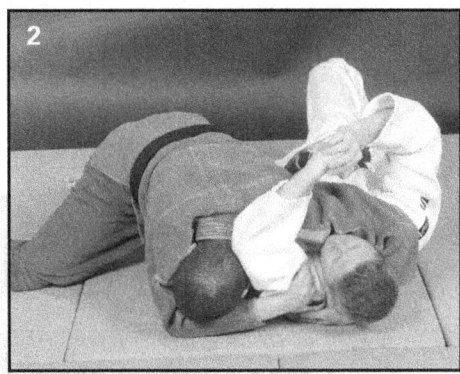
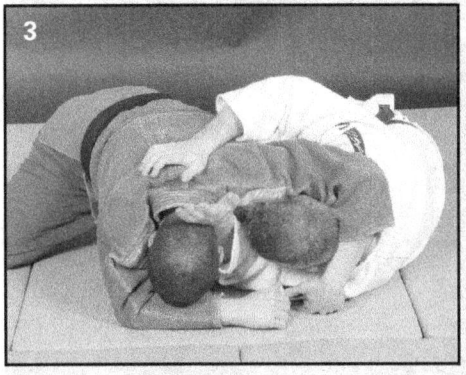

Escape Kata Gatame #2

In this escape, use the same technique to make space (see close up #1). Throw your legs over your head, locking the arm on the way over, elbow to elbow. Rotate your body for the optional arm lock.

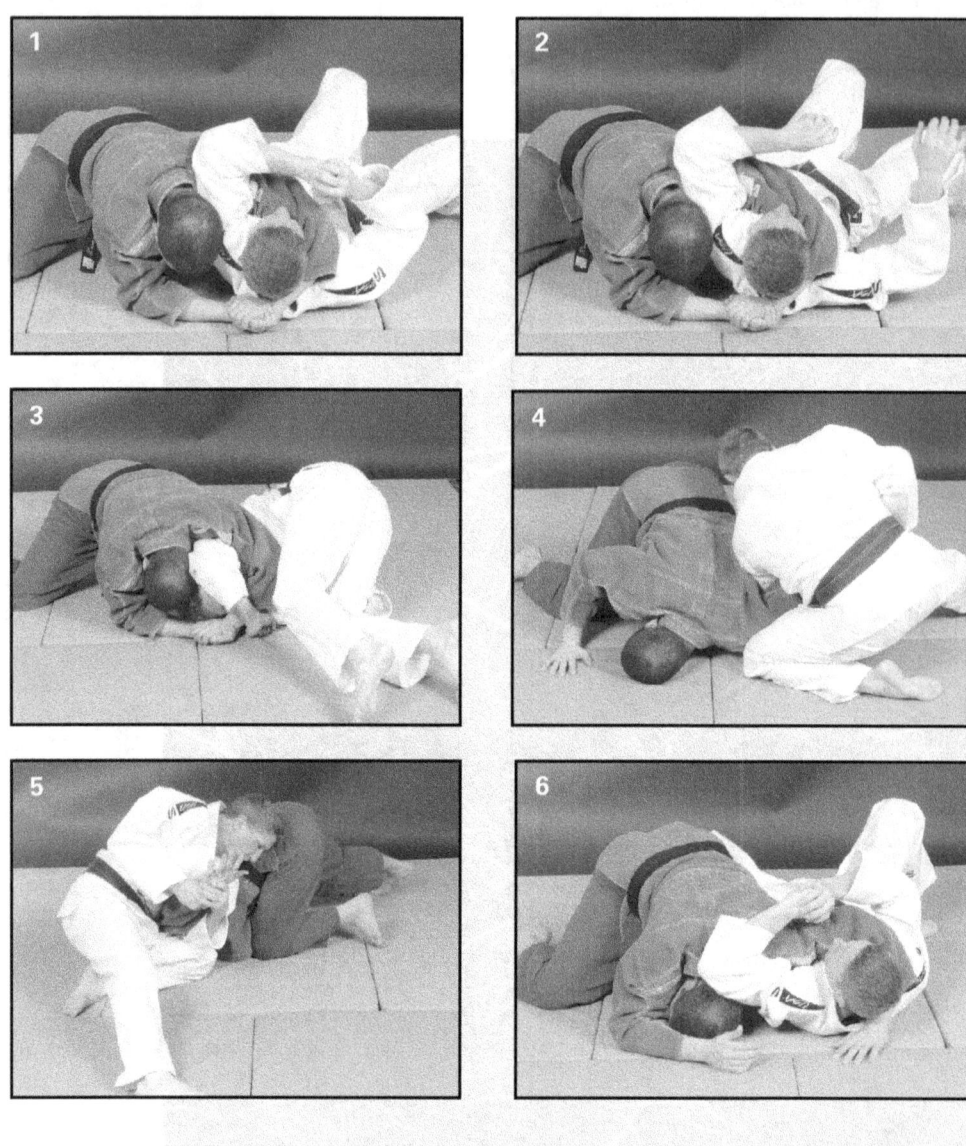

Choking Techniques

Shime—Waza (Choking Techniques)
Hand Pressure

All submission techniques of choking and arm locks should be under the strict control of the instructor at all times. It is not recommended to teach children, 12 and under, submission techniques. The signal to give up or tell your partner to stop is to tap twice on your opponent's body or the mat. The simple way to have your students understand what a choke feels like is to apply pressure against a student's neck with the sides of your wrists on each side of the carotid artery.

Do not choke them the first time. Only let them feel the pressure. Make sure you explain to them the importance and safety of tapping twice on the opponent's body to avoid injury.

Lapel Pressure

Another easy technique to help familiarize them with the technique of choking is to reach inside the lapel, thumbs and palms facing out. Your wrists should be on the carotid artery, then pull the student down into you by crossing your arms into your chest.

Again let the students feel the pressure until they tap.

Choking Technique #1
Gyaku-Juji-Jime (Cross-lock Choke) top

In this choking technique, your palms are facing upward. With the left hand, grab the left lapel, and with the right hand, grab the right lapel. Then you want to apply pressure to the neck and lean forward.

   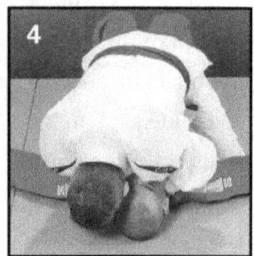

Gyaku-Juji-Jime (Cross-lock Choke) bottom

From the bottom, take the same grip, pull your opponent forward and apply the choke. Use your leg to control him as well.

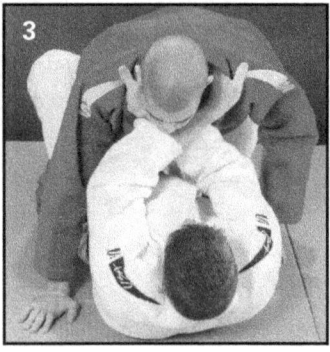 

Judo Grappling

Choking Technique #2
Kata-Ha—Jime (Single Wing Choke)

Go underneath your opponent's arm and grab the opposite lapel. Push the lapel using your thumb over to your other hand, which comes over your opponent's shoulder and around his neck. Next take your free hand and move it out to stretch his arm sideways, then come back around his head. Move your hips up toward his head and turn to your side to apply the choke.

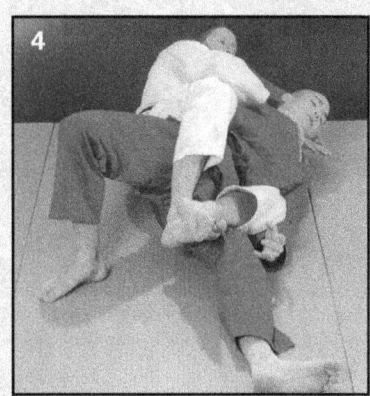

Choking Technique #3
Hadaka-Jime (Naked Arm Choke)

In this choking technique, you want to apply pressure to the neck with your bare arms. First control your opponent by using your legs to grapevine his body. Flatten your opponent forward and arch your hips to make his legs go up. Next place your thumb behind his ear and work across the neck. Clasp your hands and apply the choke by pulling in and to the side.

 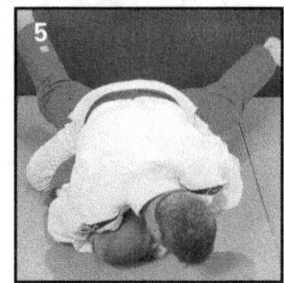

Side of neck

Direct front

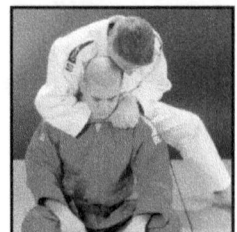

Judo Grappling

Variation #2

This time use your elbow to clear his head to the side and make space for your hand to cross the neck. Place your hand across your own elbow, then place your other hand on the back of his head to apply the choke. Squeeze in and make the circle smaller from all sides.

   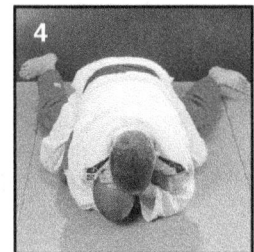

Choking Technique #4
Okuri Eri Jime Basic (Slip Choke)

This sliding collar choke is done from behind your opponent. Push or slide the collar over using your thumb (see 1). Then grab the far lapel and pull down while the hand across the throat pulls across, flexing your wrist out. The key to remember here is the lapel hand pulling down is the one choking and not so much the collar hand across the neck. When your opponent reaches up to pull your hand down off his neck, keep applying pressure with the lapel hand pulling down. It is also important to control your opponent with your legs as grapevines. Keep pushing your opponent down your body away from your chest to execute the choke.

Championship Judo

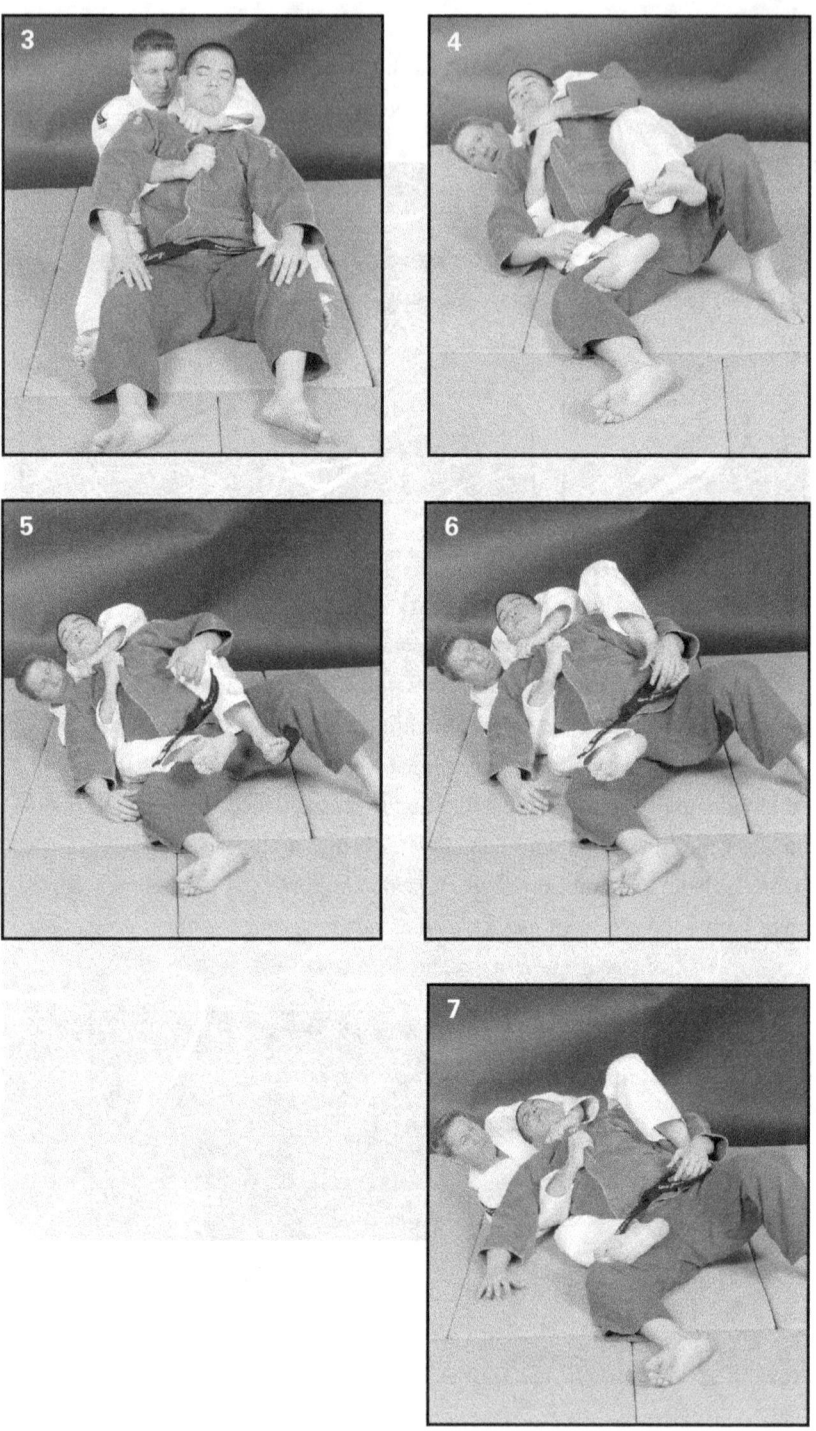

Judo Grappling

Okuri Eri Jime Variation #1 (Slip Choke From Top)

This choke can also be applied from the top. First, control your opponent using your weight with your chest on the middle of your opponent's back (see close up #1) for proper placement of the hands. Jump out in front, pulling across with the collar grip and down with the lapel. Switch your legs and sit through, keeping your hips low to the ground.

Okuri Eri Jime Variation #2 (Slip Choke Roll)

Another variation of okuri eri jime is to trap your opponent's arm from the top and roll through. Make sure you push your opponent down off your chest after you roll to complete the choke. You can also use your leg to tighten the choke.

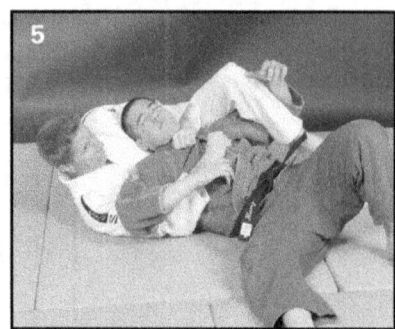

Okuri Eri Jime Counter

To counter a choke always keep your chin down, look toward your opponent's arm and pull down. Push all your weight onto your opponent's chest and slide your hips through for a reverse kesa gatame pin.

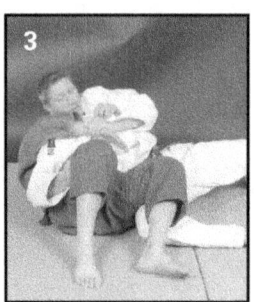
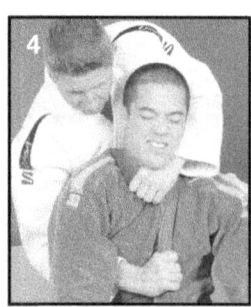

Judo Grappling

Choking Technique #5
San Gaku Jime—Basic (From Top)

The crucial thing to remember is san gaku jime means triangle choke. Your legs must form a triangle with your opponent's head and arm inside. When your opponent attacks standing and then falls into the turtle position (see 1 below), grab your opponent's collar and belt, pulling your opponent forward to make space for your heel to enter behind his elbow. Touch your heel to your knee to make the triangle. Slide your belt hand over and use as a gut wrench to pull your opponent to his side. The first move when you are on your side is to pull the far arm across and tighten the triangle by squeezing your knees together. Lock the arm closest to you with your hand (see close up A on page 129). Then you can tie up this arm and control it using his belt or gi (see close up #2 & #3 on page 129).

To apply a shoulder lock against your opponent's top arm, push away from your opponent's body, keeping his arm close to your leg (see close up #4 on page 129). Another option is to come up for the pin by placing your hand down (see #5 on page 129) on the mat and sliding your body to the opposite side for a side mount with the tie up.

Triangle

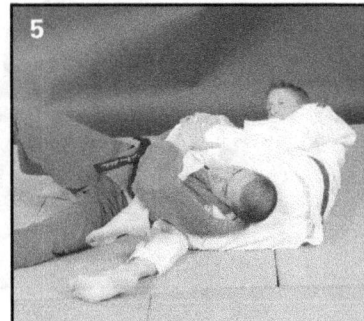
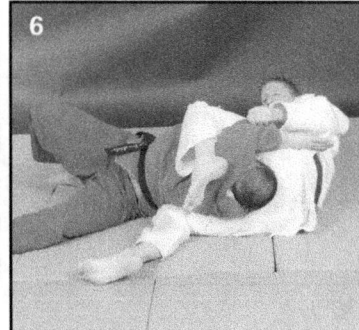

Championship Judo

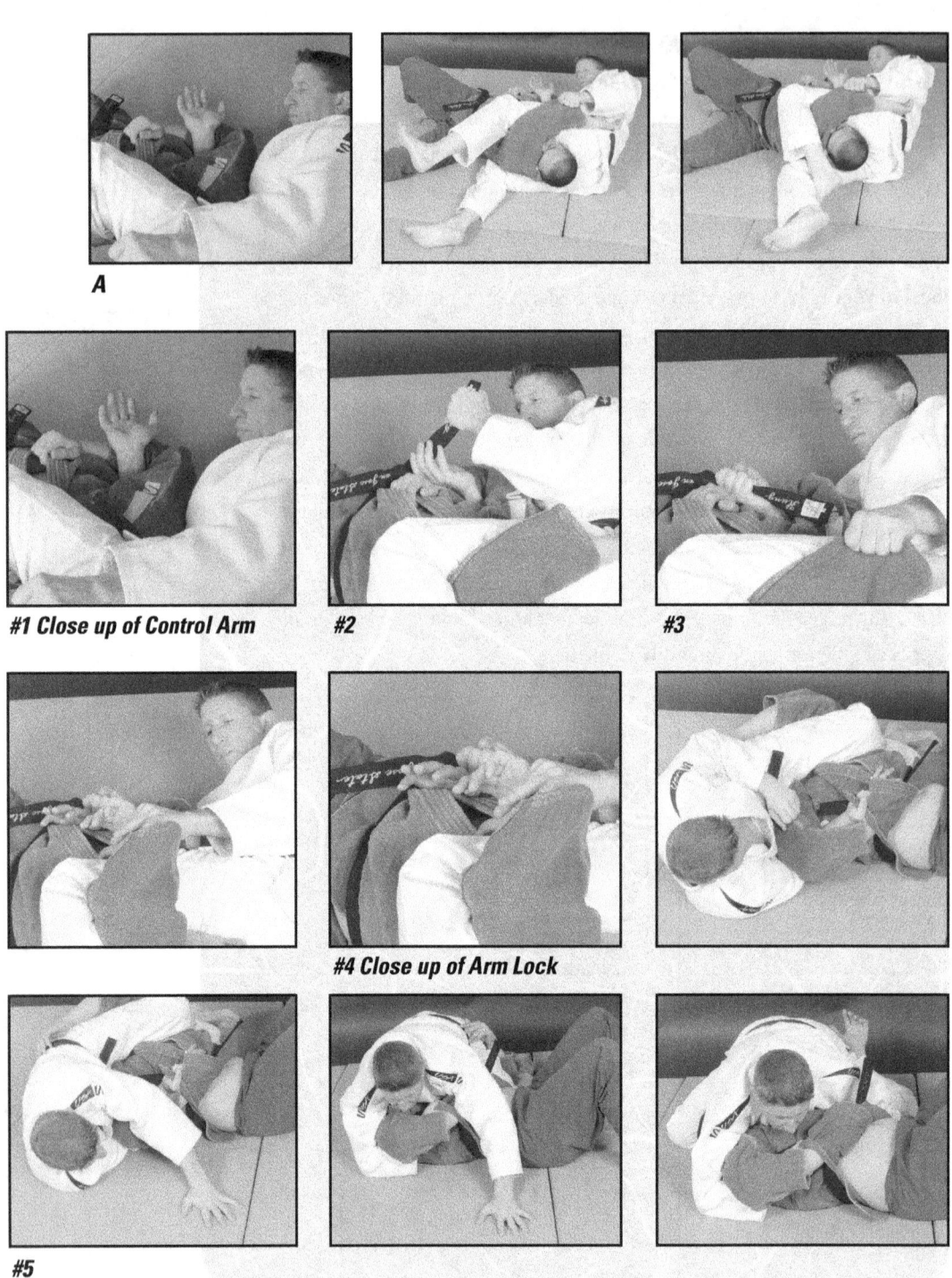

A

#1 Close up of Control Arm

#2

#3

#4 Close up of Arm Lock

#5

Judo Grappling

Escape San Gaku Jime

In defending against the triangle choke it is critical not to let your opponent get the triangle in tight. Block the incoming heel with your hand and the knee with your other hand (see 2). As your opponent rolls, push the opposite way and spin through.

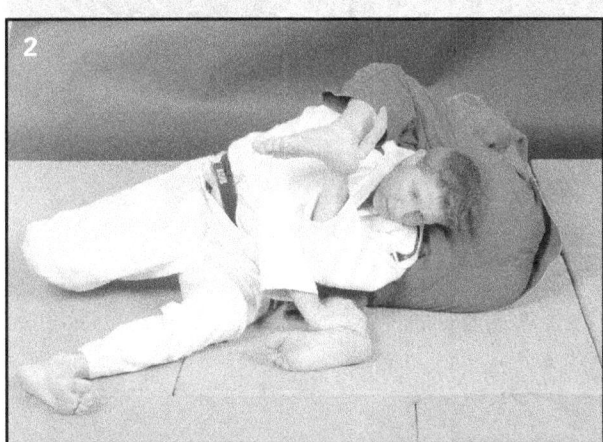

Championship Judo

San Gaku Variation #1 (Roll to Other Side)

In this variation, once you secure the triangle, roll the other way. Pull your opponent's far leg toward your head so you flip your opponent over your body into the standard san gaku position. From this point everything is the same; reach across and pull your opponent's top arm to you to secure the hold and from there choke, pin, or arm lock.

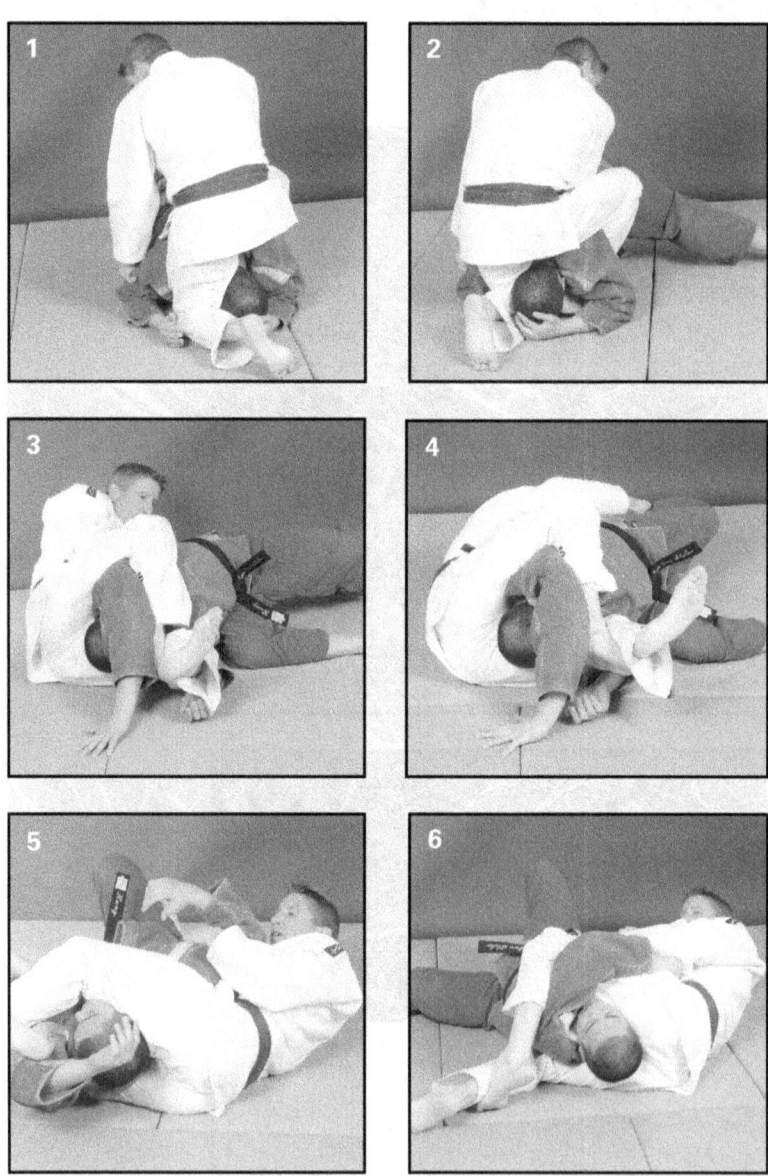

Judo Grappling

San Gaku Variation #2 (Roll Over Back)

In this variation your opponent stands up as you lock in the triangle. Using your opponent's momentum, roll forward and through, ending up in the same side position with the triangle choke.

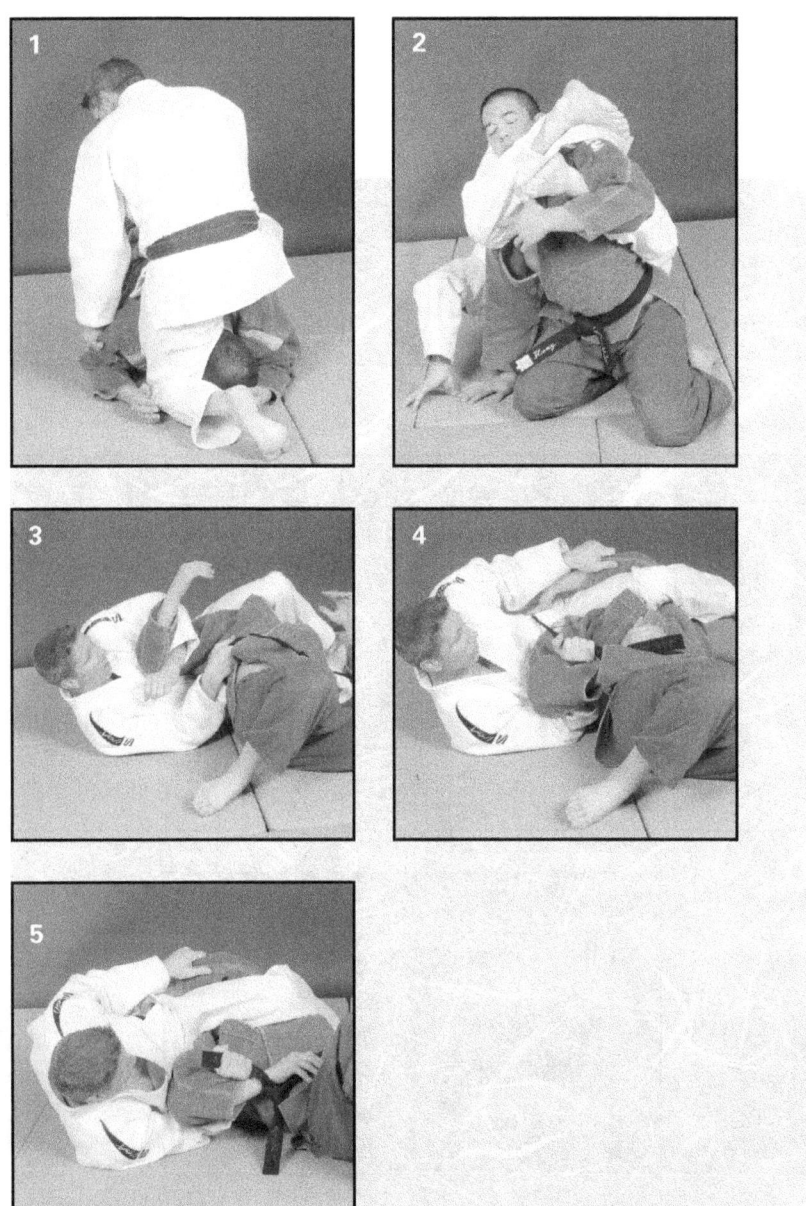

Championship Judo

San Gaku Jime #6 (From Bottom)

This same triangle choke is shown from the bottom. The important point to remember here is to bring your hips off the mat and pull your opponent's arm across your body to get a good tight triangle lock. Once your opponent falls to their side you have the option to choke by squeezing your knees together or arm lock by extending your hips forward.

Pull Arm Across Body

From Bottom Triangle

Armlock Techniques

Kansetsu-Waza (Arm Locks)

Safety is the most important feature in arm locks. Make sure your students understand that if they tap twice, this will release the pressure from their opponent. This is called the "tap out" and it is the best way to prevent your students from getting injured.

Arm lock Technique #1
Ude-Garame (Entangled Arm Lock)
Top position

Let's look at the basis of ude-garame from the side position. The arms extended, get a figure four, pull the elbow in and then up. The elbow, most importantly, must come into the opponent's body. Again, figure four, in and up. As we take a look without the uniform we can how the elbow is entangled and the arm lock is actually already applied as you pull it in, but then when you pull it up, it applies even more pressure.

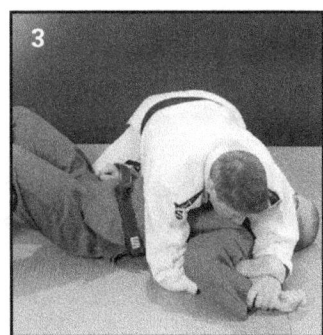

Championship Judo

Ude Garame—Bottom Position

Now let's look at the same technique, but with the arm in a different position. This time, you're going to reach out and grab his wrist with your right hand, pull the arm in and behind his back. You're still figure four, in and up. Without the uniform, figure four, in and up. Lift your weight up to make space and apply the arm lock behind your opponent's back.

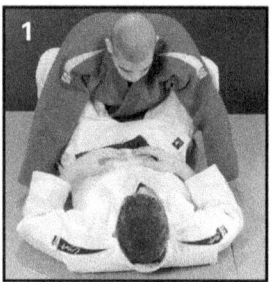  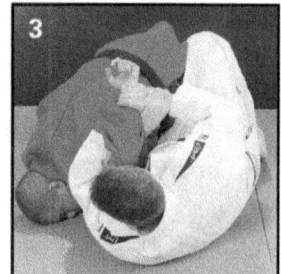

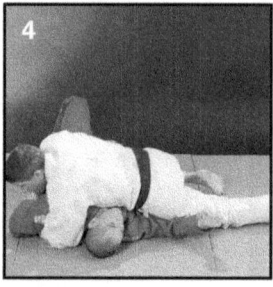 

Arm lock Technique #2
Ude Gatame (straight lock)
Top Position

As your opponent reaches up to choke, cup the back of his elbow and trap his hand against your neck. Pull your partner's elbow straight into your body and keep your back straight. Lift your knee up next to his/her head and pull arm to your chest.

 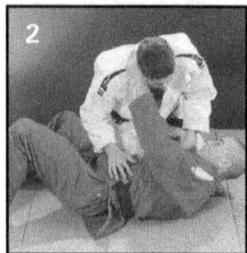 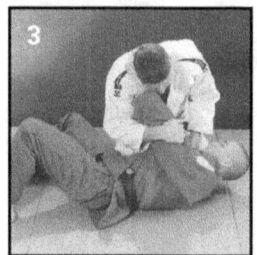 

Judo Grappling

Ude Gatame—Bottom Position

As your opponent is attacking from between your legs, place your four fingers behind his/her elbow. Reach across and over with your opposite hand and straighten his/her arm. The most important thing about this move is to shoot your hips out and turn to your side to apply pressure.

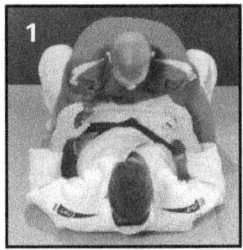  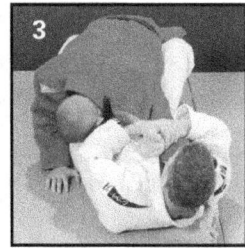 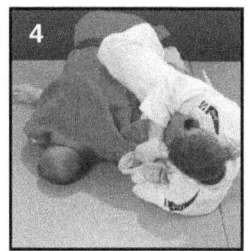

Arm lock Technique #3
Juji-Gatame (Cross Body Lock)

As you step over his head, the most important thing is to squeeze your knees together. Control his body with your knees and legs squeezed together. Keep your backside close to his shoulder. There can't be any space between his arm and your backside. As you pull down on the arm, arch your hips up for maximum pressure. As you sit, stay close to his body. The most important thing in this arm lock is to control the head and the arm by squeezing your knees together. When the arm is extended the pinkie finger goes down with thumb up to control his wrist.

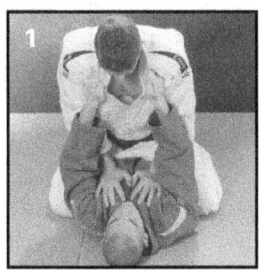 

Championship Judo

Methods of releasing the arm

The basic rule to remember is the direction of the release is first toward the head then 90%. The pinky points to the floor, knees squeeze together and control head and body.

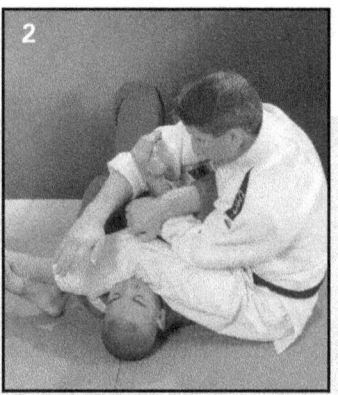
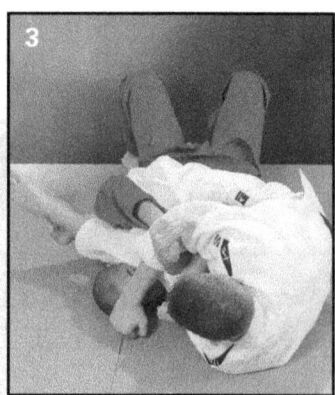

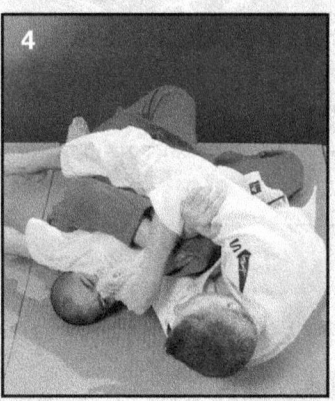

Judo Grappling

Arm lock Technique #4
Hiza Gatame (Knee Arm Lock)

Control your opponent with a cross collar and sleeve grip. Pull toward you while placing your foot on your opponent's far hip to extend her body. Shifting your hip to one side, bring your knee over, trapping her shoulder and arm. Pinch your opponent's wrist between your head and shoulder, applying pressure on the elbow joint.

Arm lock Technique #5
Hara Gatame (Stomach Arm Lock)

This is a very quick and effective move because it is difficult to see it coming. Hook the closest arm with your leg closest to your opponent's feet. Use your stomach and hips to keep your opponent's head down while extending the arm. Figure-four your legs in order to control the arm. You may have to adjust slightly side to side in order to apply the arm lock.

Judo Grappling

Grappling Combinations

Okuri Eri Jime to Juji Gatame (Choke to Arm Lock)

The key to this combination is surprise. Quickly push your opponent's head away (see 4) to separate his head from his shoulder, giving you space to bring your leg up and over the head. Quickly bring your knees together in order to tighten the cross body arm lock on juji gatame.

  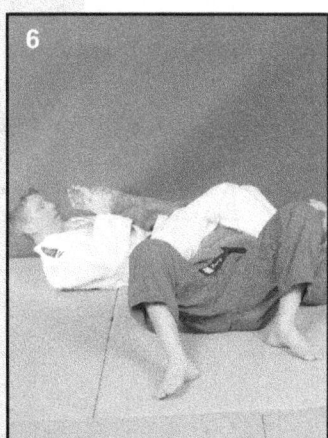

Championship Judo

Kata Gatame to Juji Gatame (Shoulder Hold to Arm Lock)

As your opponent turns out to escape the hold down, scoop the arm and bring your opponent's elbow to your chest. Then sit back into juji gatame.

Grappling Turnovers

Side Roll (Arm Hook Turnover)

The small secret to this turnover is to bump your opponent away from you (see A). This will cause your opponent to react and push back, which is when you pull her far hip to you. Once she is on her side, cup her biceps, keeping your elbow deep behind her back (see close up B and C). Keeping your hips low, roll your opponent back into a pin.

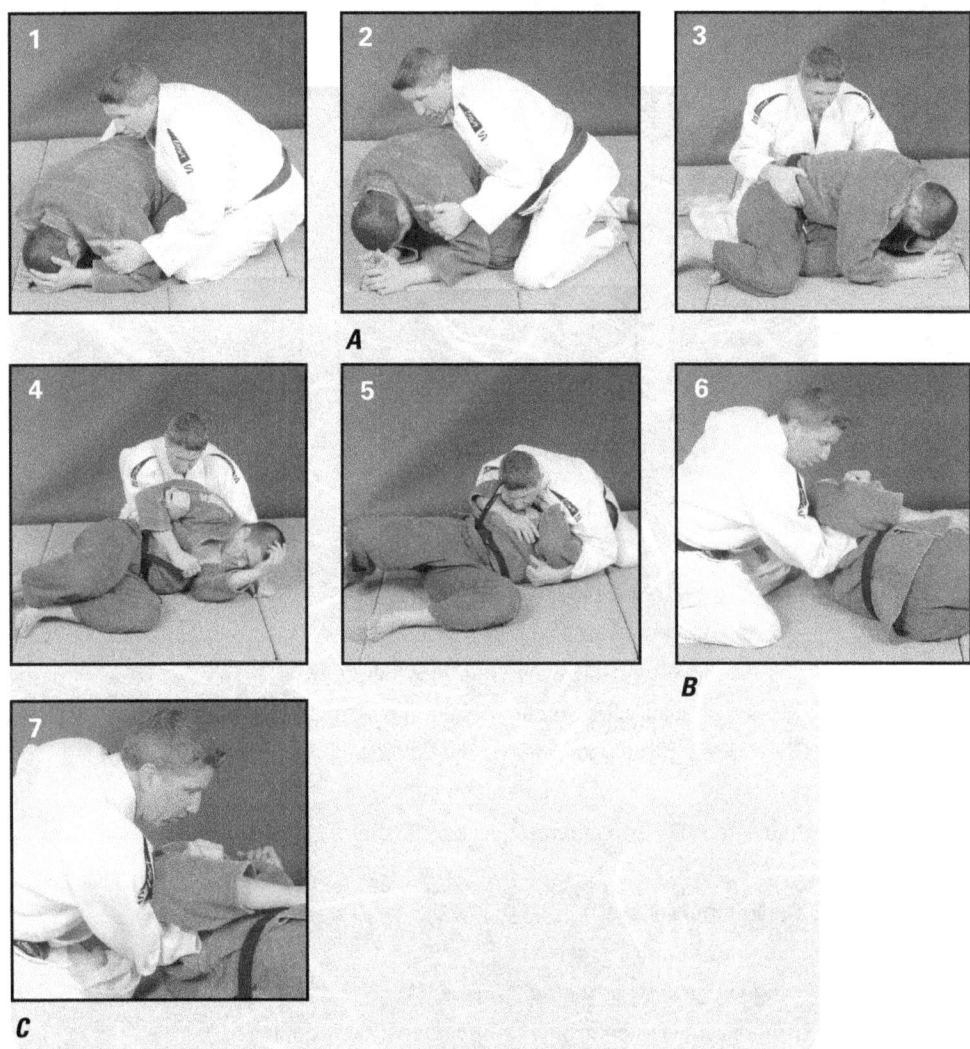

Championship Judo

Side Rollover (Trap Body With Elbow)

Start in the same position as the side roll arm hook, controlling your opponent's shoulder and keeping your leg tucked close to his leg. As you roll, grab the far lapel to pull. Trap your opponent's arm by grabbing the belt and keeping your elbow down, as well as your knee down on his hip (see 5). Throw your legs back and keep your hips down for the pin.

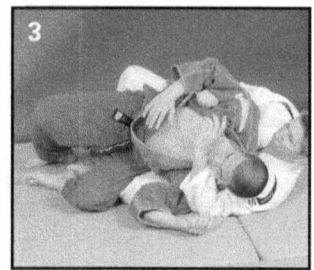
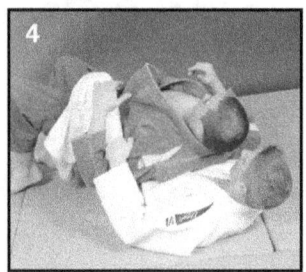

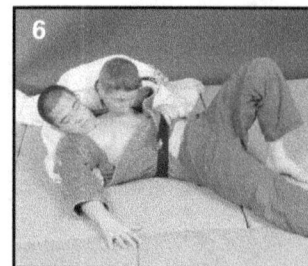

Arm Pry (Thread Needle Turnover)

As you are working a choke reach in and grab the closest wrist. Swing your body out to the side, keeping all your weight on your opponent's elbow. Next, place your knee on the far side of your opponent's head so she cannot slide away. Figure-four her arm and roll over for the pin.

The key points are:
Turn your thumb up (see A)
Bring your elbow to your chest (see B)
Use your knee to control your opponent's shoulder (see C).

Judo Grappling

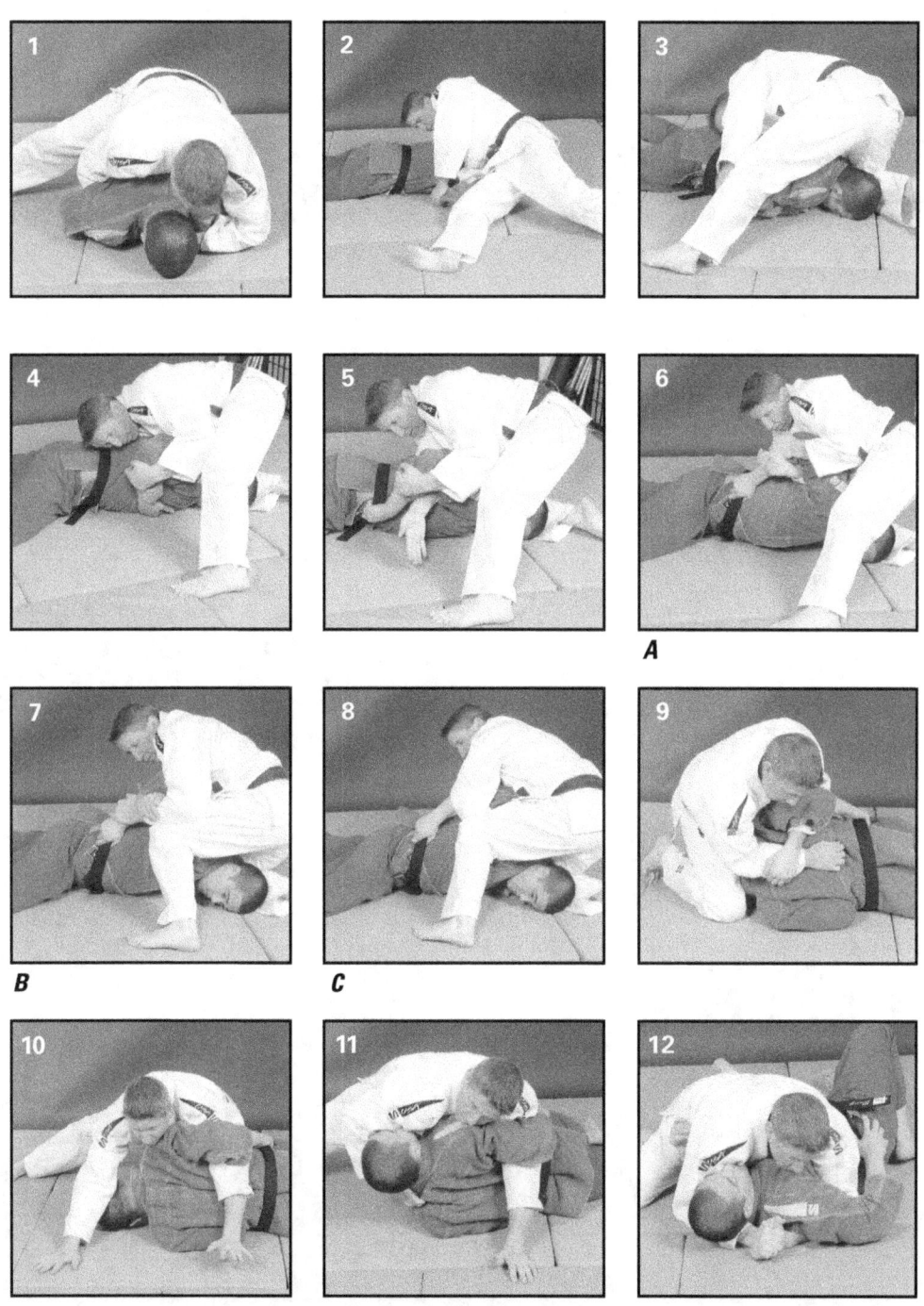

145

Chapter 4

Competitive Judo

Competitive Gripping

There are two basic stances in Judo that I refer to my descriptions of the techniques: ai-yotsu (same sided grips) and kenka-yotsu (different sided grips). My natural stance is left sided because I put my left foot forward. Therefore, when I fight a left sided player this is considered ai-yotsu or same sided grip; left vs. left. In my opinion, the most important grip in competition is the sleeve hand of the opponent or hikite (pulling hand). Without this grip, it is difficult to pull your opponent off balance. With this *hikite* you can control the grip game and put your opponent on the defense. The lapel grip (tsurite) literally translated means *fishing hand*, because of the lifting wrist action, which lifts your opponent to their toes. Keep in mind that the more you keep the two hands gripping on your opponent (hikite and tsurite), the higher number of possibilities you have to throw and counter throws. Fighting with one hand is limiting your chances to score as well as making you more vulnerable to be thrown. Also, a straight up body posture is still important to maintaining balance yourself in order to off balance and throw your opponent.

In the modern competitive Judo, gripping has many variations and continues to evolve showing new variations and entries to throws. Grip fighting is fierce and can break fighters mentally, however most champions at the top always seem to keep two hands gripping and controlling rather then playing the grip breaking game. Pictures 1–24 show various legal and illegal gripping techniques.

Illegal competition grips and stance

Defensive posture 1, 2, & 4 are illegal if you do not attack within 5 seconds.

Illegal uniform grip (3) (fingers inside opponent's pants)

Pistol grip—holding the opponent's sleeves end(s) between the thumb and the fingers 14 & 15.

Two on one side—Two hands gripping one sleeve side – must attack in 5 seconds or two hands on one lapel – must attack in 5 seconds (11, 16, 18, & 22).

Competitive Judo

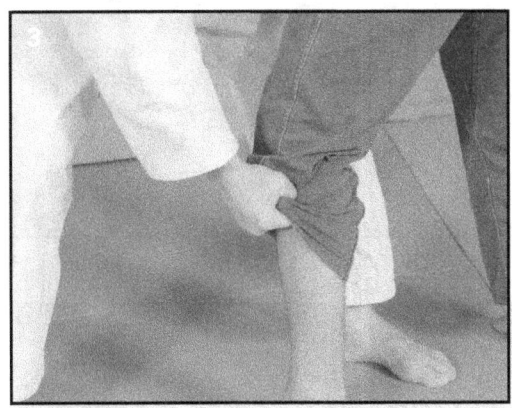
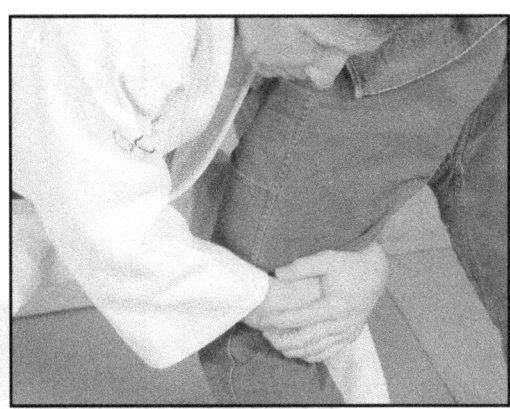

Defensive Grips

Back grip The grip in pictures 12, 17, 19, & 21 is legal, but you need to attack in 5 seconds.

Ducking your head—Opponent starts with standard legal grip (20). Then opponent dips his head to avoid a high collar grip. Now the grip is illegal and you have 5 seconds to attack or the opponent may get penalized for dipping head. This is a subjective call by the referee.

Belt Grip—Holding opponent's belt is legal (8) but you have to attack in 5 seconds.

Championship Judo

Examples of Gripping

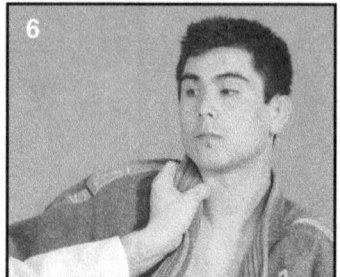
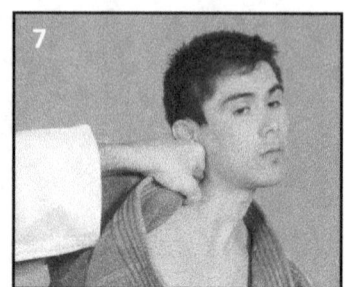

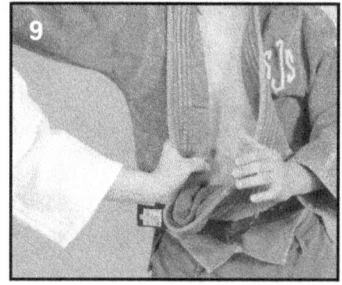

Classic Grip

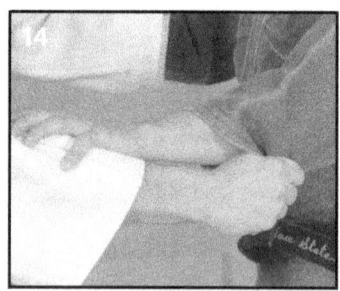

Pistol Grip, illegal

Competitive Judo

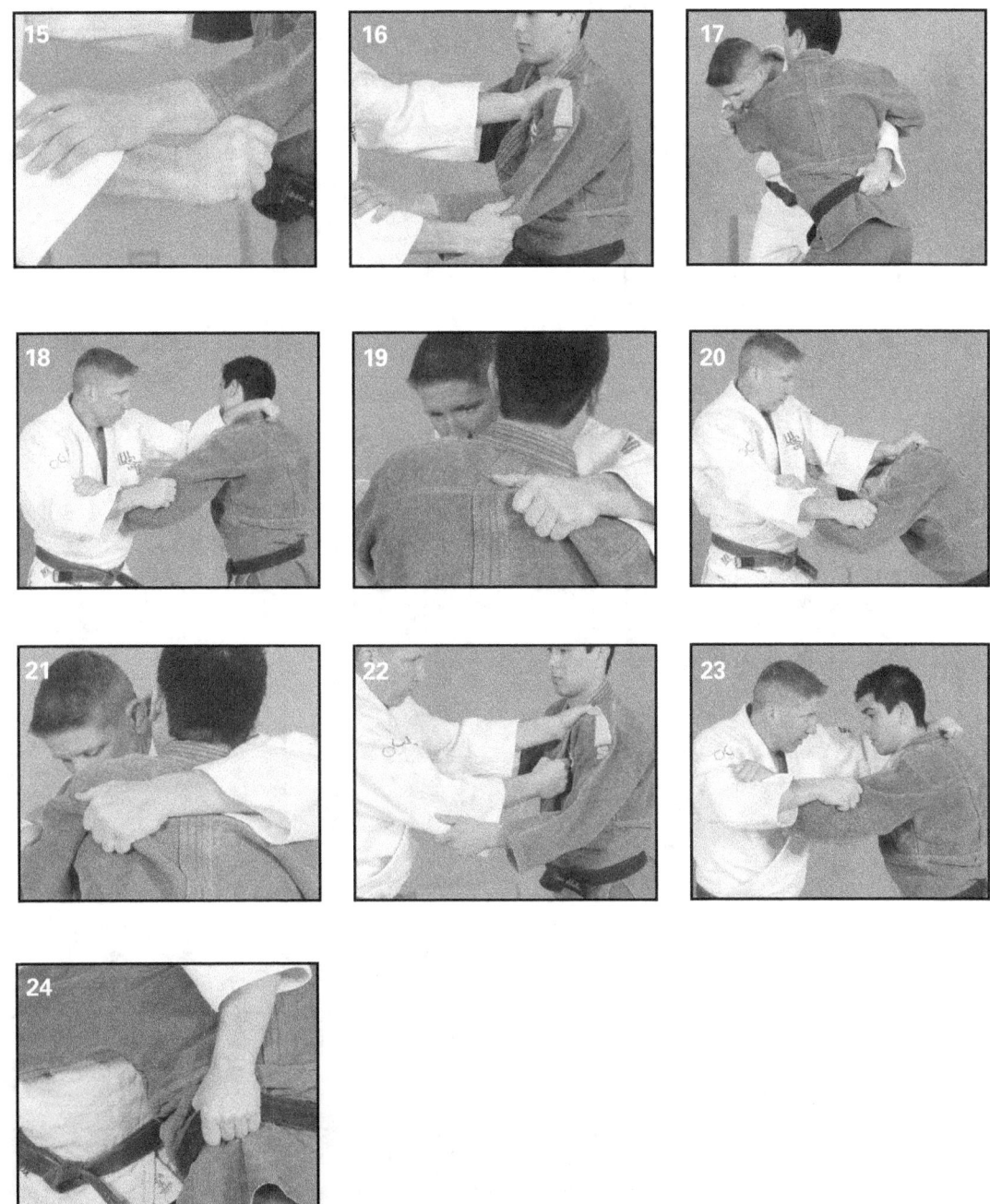

151

Variation to Tai Otoshi (side body drop) with one hand

From a same side stance (1), block the action with two hands (2). Grab the sleeve with one hand and turn into the opponent collapsing your other hand into your body using it as a support for the throw (3).

Breaking the standard same side lapel grip

Starting with a standard grip (1), place your left hand on top of opponent's wrist (2). Push straight down with your body while arching your back (3). Continue this motion with small jerks until opponent lets go of his grip (4), and control the sleeve grip regaining the lapel grip (5).

Competitive Judo

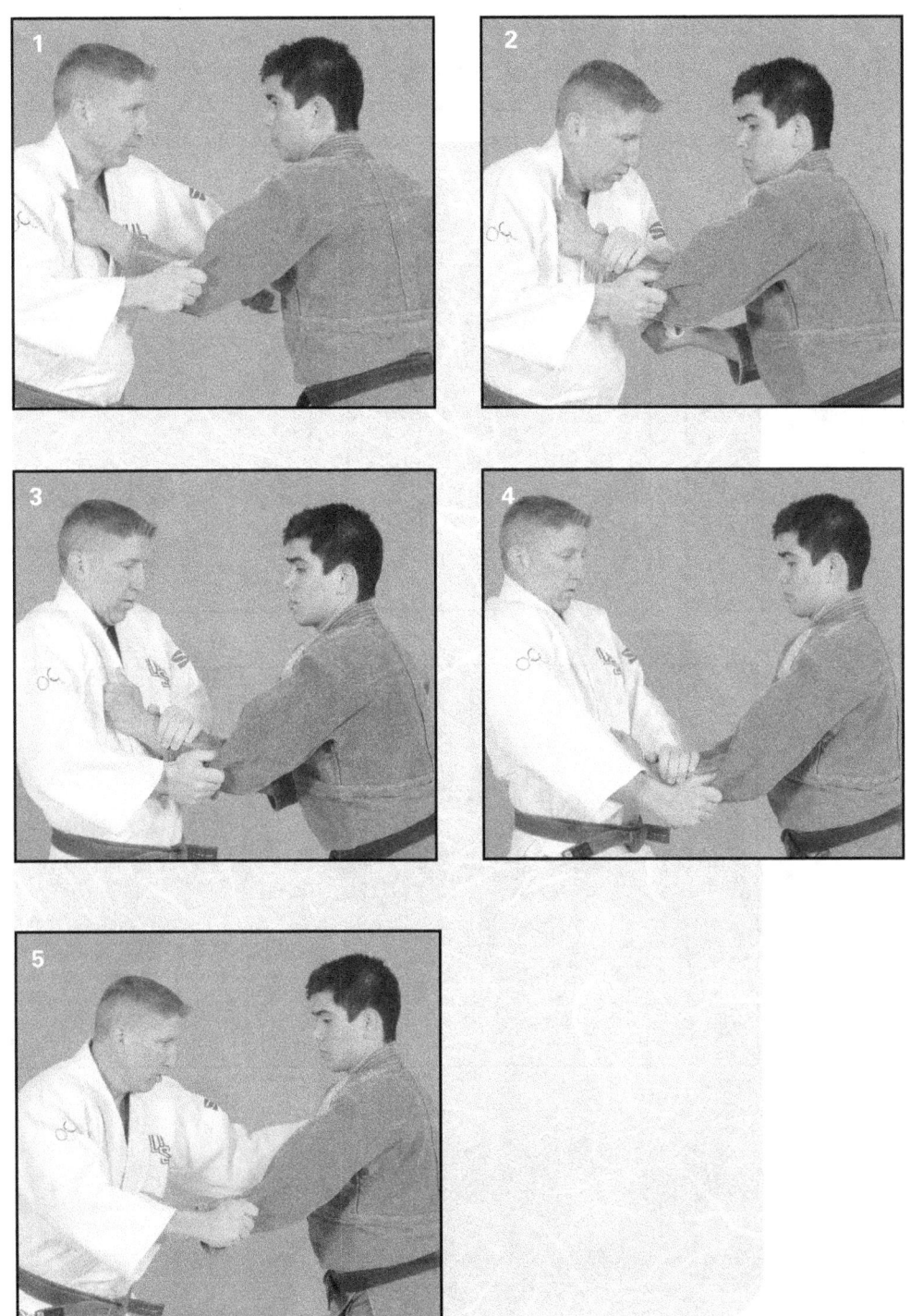

153

Breaking the high collar with side grip

Starting form a high collar grip (1), place your left hand on opponent's inside sleeve (2). Then, push away and arch your back (3). Continue to push and arch (4). Push sleeve down to control before reaching back for lapel (5). (Page 155, photo 6.)

Competitive Judo

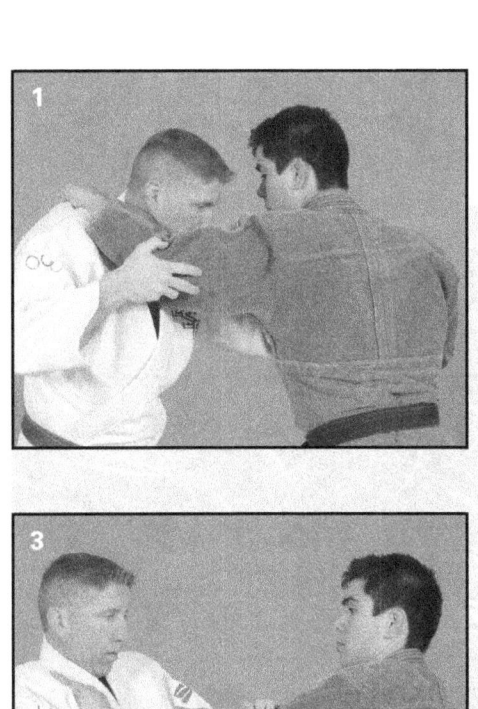

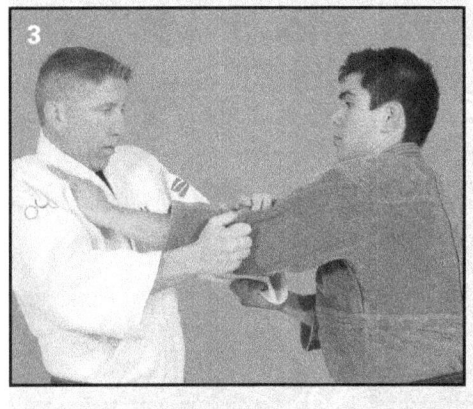

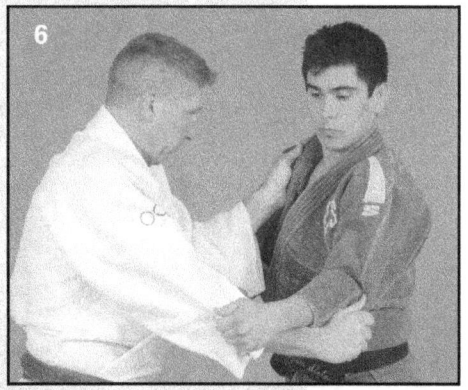

Breaking the sleeve grip against standard same side grip.

Starting from the same side grip (1), reach over and gain control of opponent's lapel closest to your sleeve grip and hold both lapels (2). Then, push his shoulder back and break free with your other arm (3 &4). Re-grip the lapel (5), and maintain a stronger basic grip.

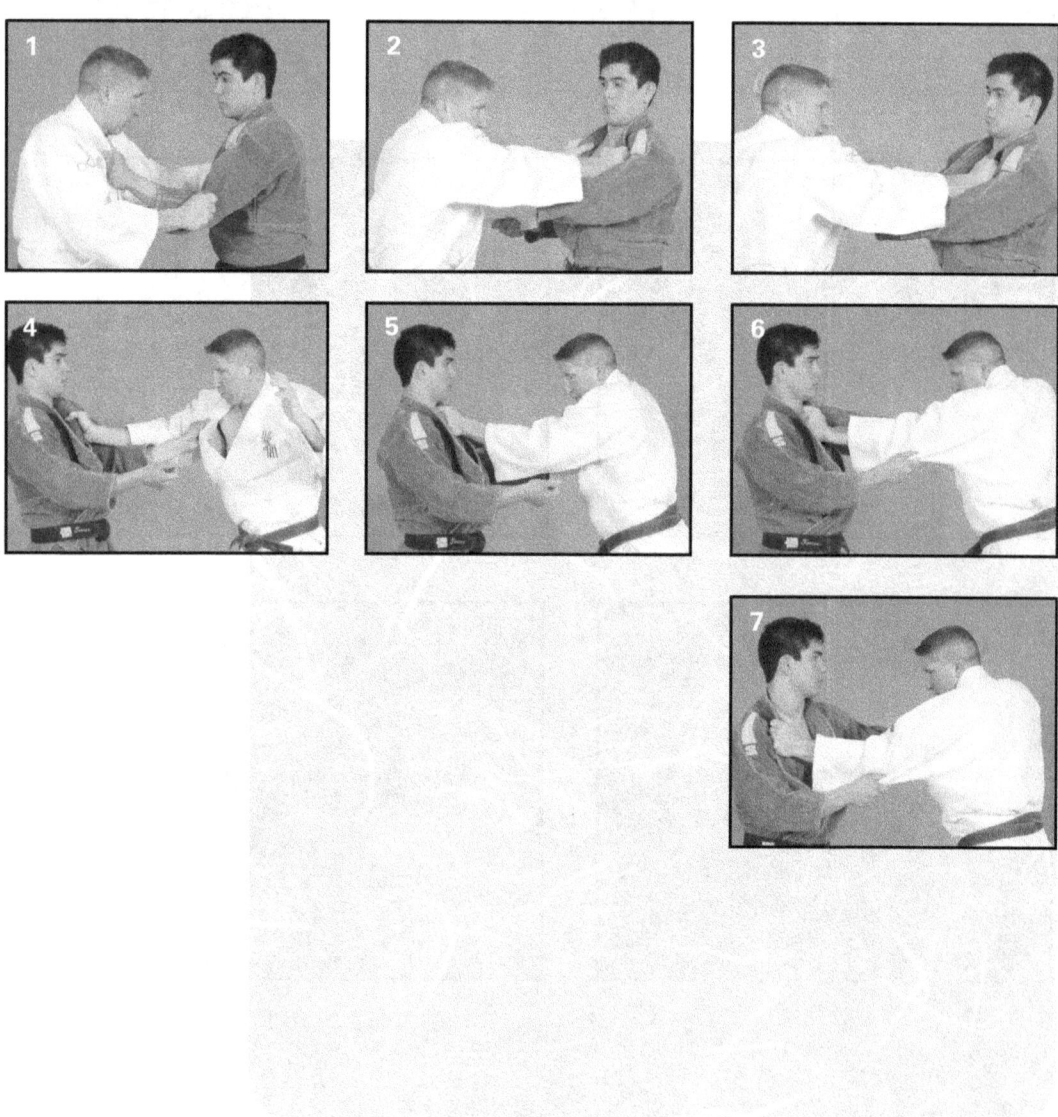

Competitive Judo

Controlling the sleeve against same side grip

The key to grip fighting is to control the sleeve for pulling the opponent off balance. Therefore, if the opponent's sleeve hand is out take it with two hands (1&2), because you need to stay balanced. Don't reach for the lapel. Push it to the side and grab the closer lapel (3&4). Maintain a two-lapel grip and pull them closer to you (5). Then, you can re-grip the sleeve for a complete grip.

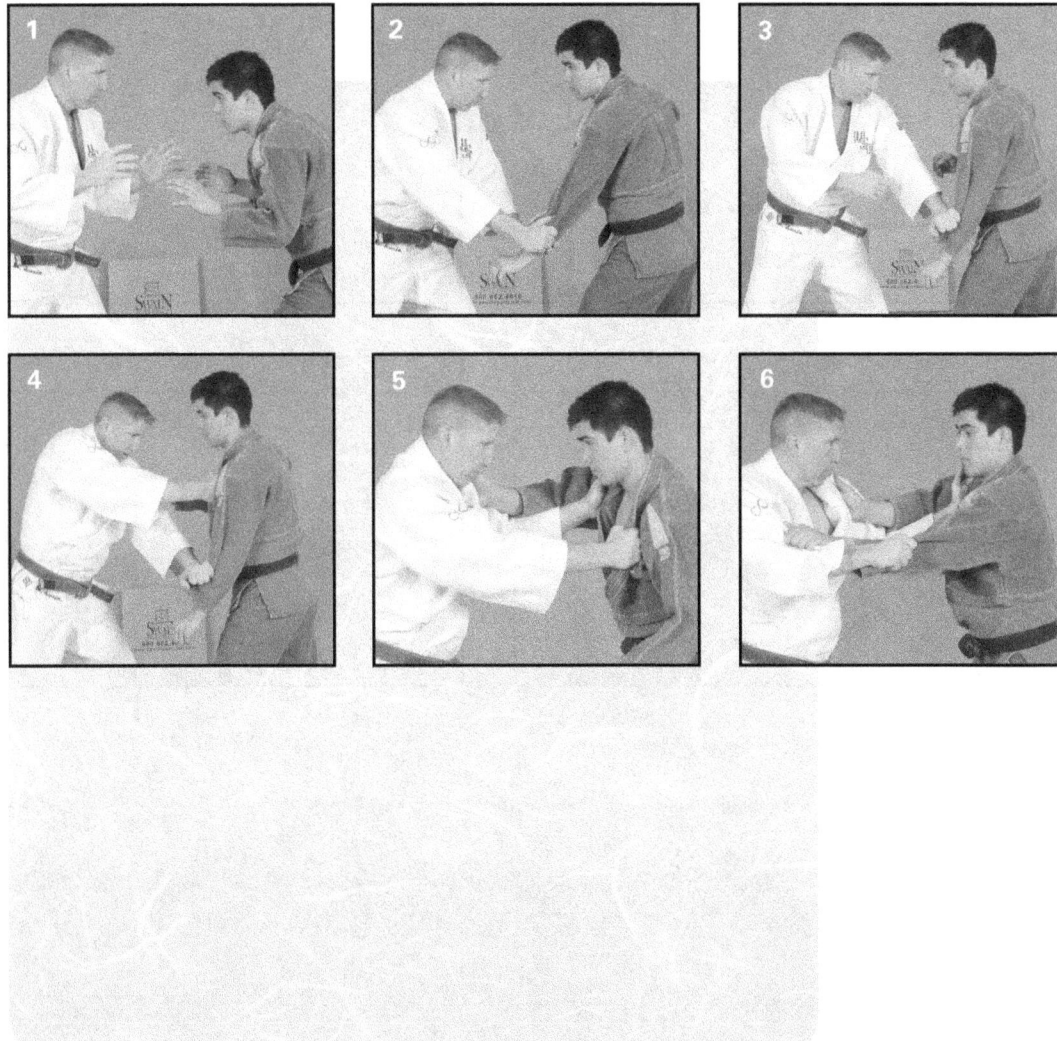

Stopping the opposite side grip

Start by standing square to your opponent and control the closest shoulder first (1). Then, take the inside grip at the opponents collar bone area (2), control the sleeve (3), and immediately throw your opponent off balance by pulling the sleeve toward you (4).

Competitive Judo

Stopping the opposite side high grip

When facing an opposite side high grip (1), use both hands to stop the opponent at the shoulder and mid-arm (2). Then, control the sleeve pushing it to the side and down (3). Maintain the inside lapel grip (4), and regain your basic grip (5).

Championship Judo

Defense against opposite side high grip

If your opponent has a secure high grip (1), use your hand against the neck to create space (2). While standing up push away (3), and turn you outside shoulder away by taking a strong stance. Then, twist your lapel grip in a punching motion (4). Use the palm of your hand to push his wrist off (5) and regain your basic grip (6).

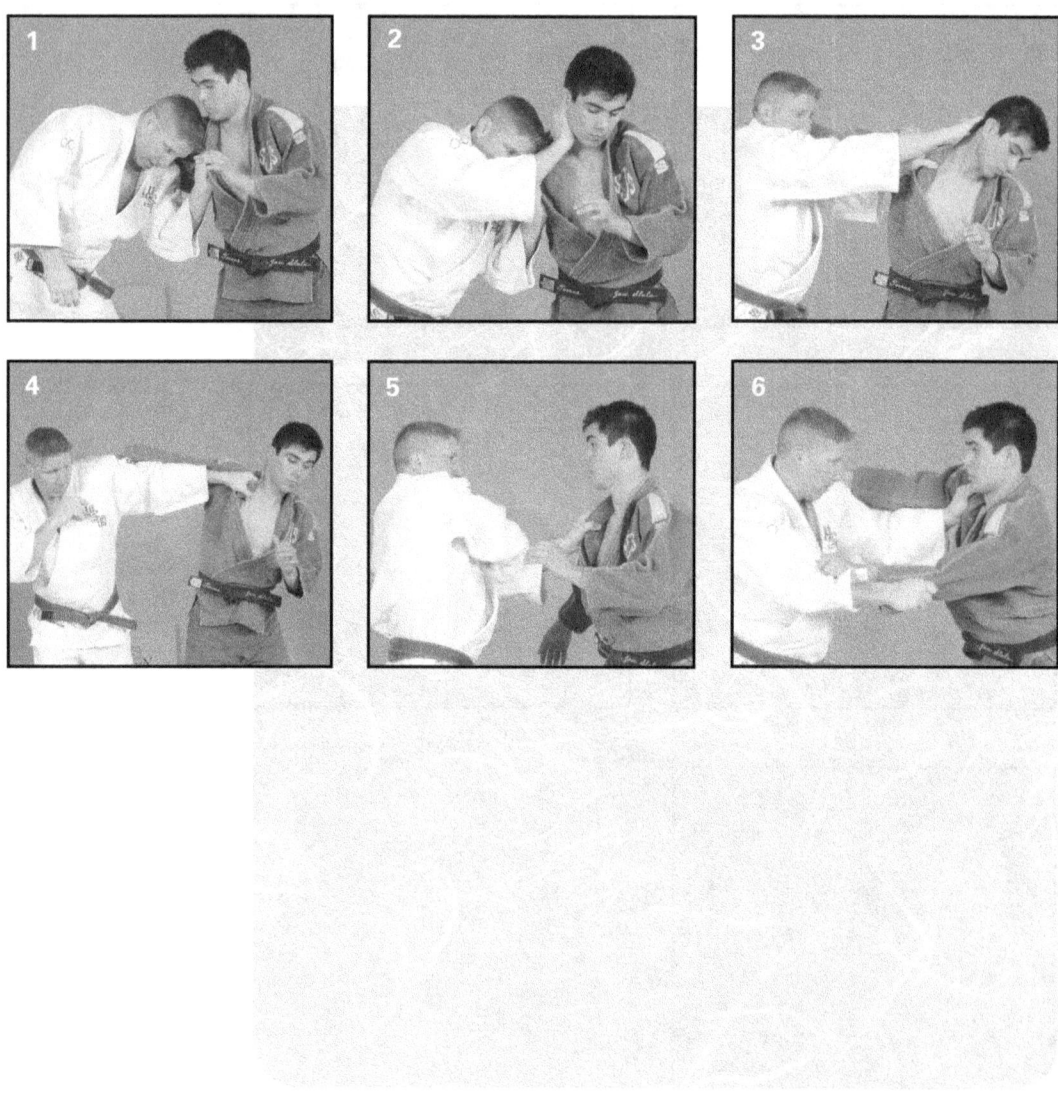

Competitive Judo

Defense against back grip opposite side

If your opponent has a deep back grip (1), straighten your posture and arm by twisting your lapel hand in a punching motion (2). Continue this motion against opponent's chin until he is off balance (3). Close up (B). Then, maintain your basic sleeve grip (4). It is important to maintain good posture and not to reach for the sleeve grip but pull your body in closer with a small step (5 & 6).

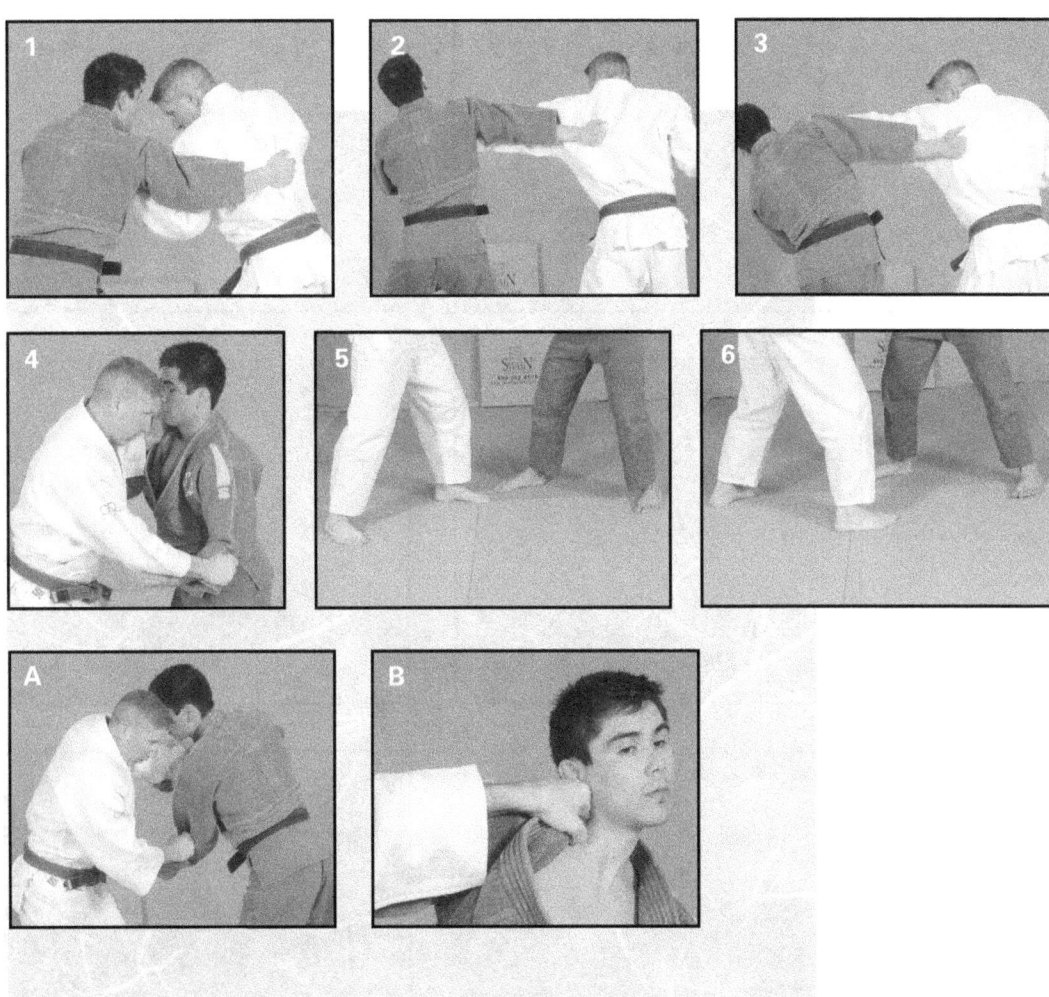

Controlling the same side high grip

When fighting with a high grip (1), use your wrist to pull down your opponent (2 & 3). Then, as your opponent tries to stand up (4), pull him forward until he is off balance and attack (5). The key point is to make your opponent feel uncomfortable and lose his concentration. This is the correct time to attack.

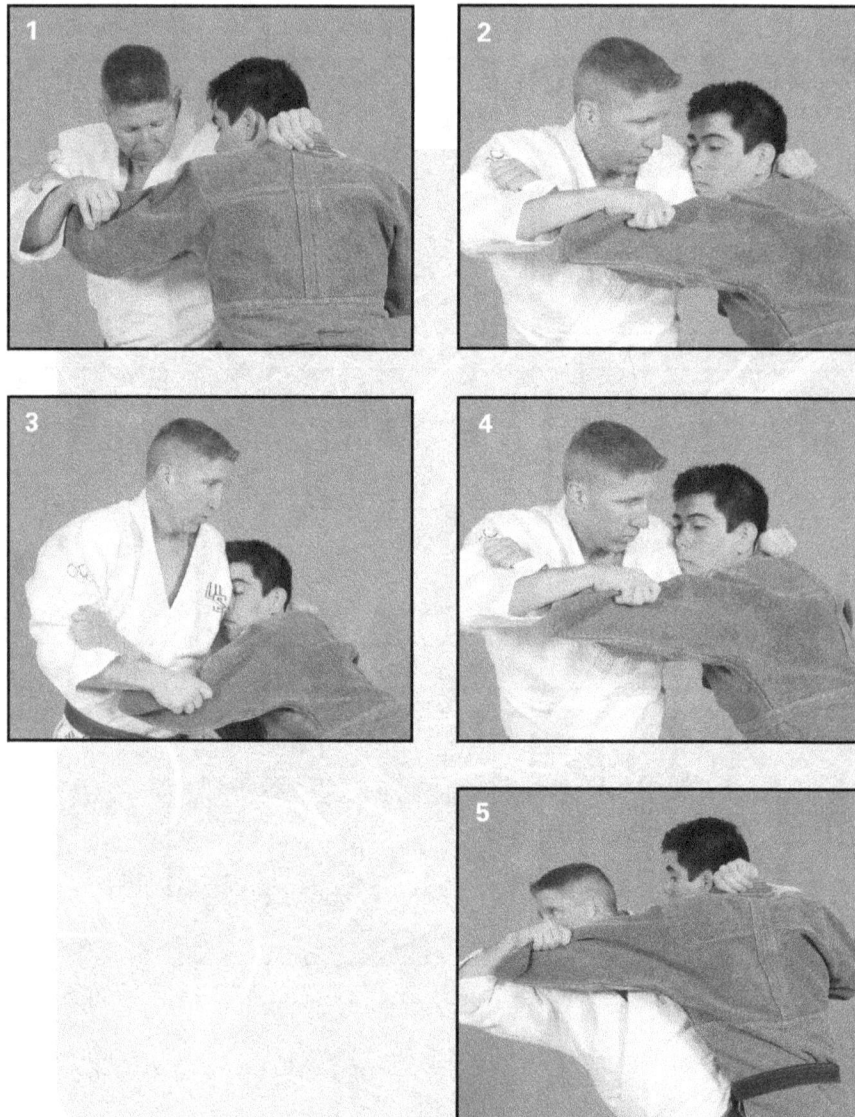

Competitive Judo

Stopping the same side high grip

If you stop the shoulder your opponent cannot turn in for the same side throw (1). Block the arm and secure an inside grip (2). Then, push his body away to create space (3), and take a strong basic grip (4).

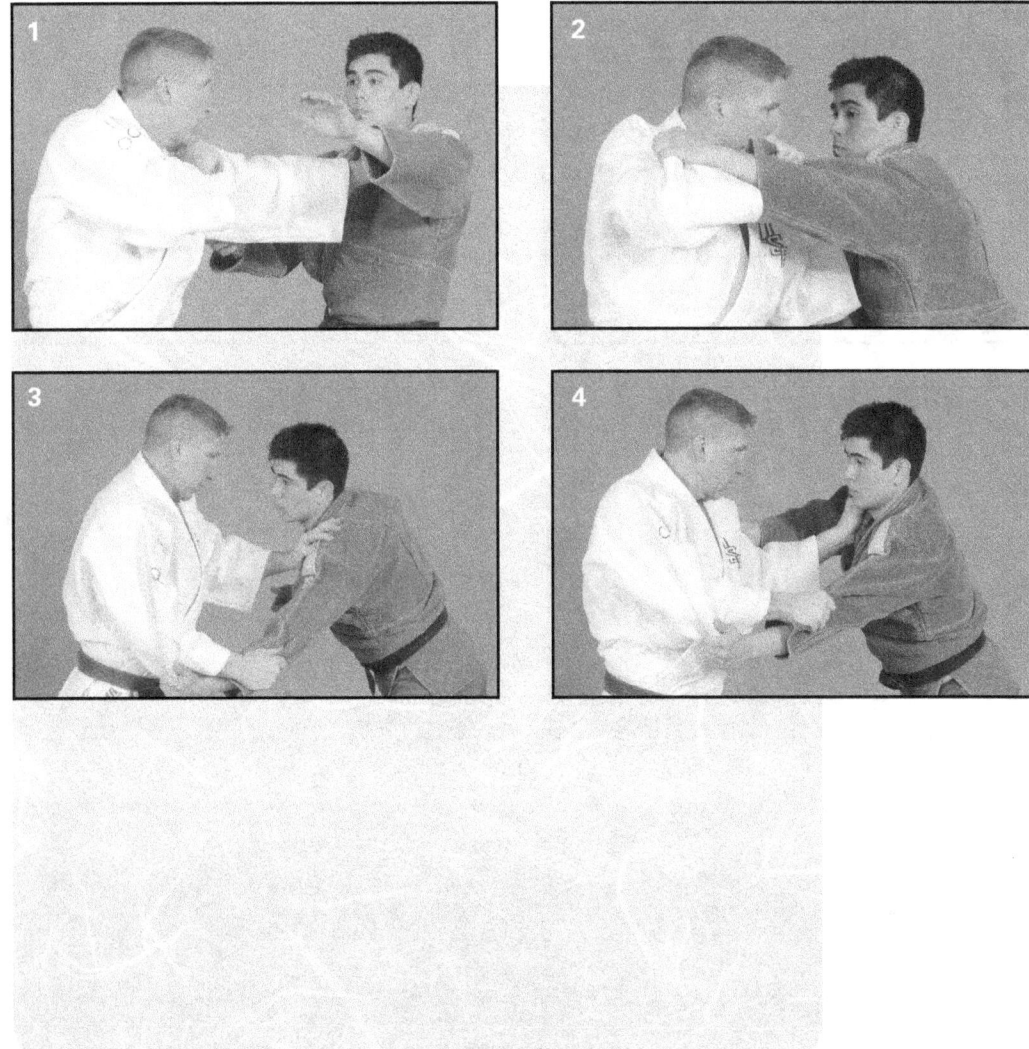

Controlling the leading elbow it side grip

From the same side grip (1), break the grip off by pushing down and arching up slightly (2). Immediately, push the sleeve into and across opponent's body (3), as he reacts by pulling his elbow back out attack for the rear throw (4). By applying a corkscrew type pressure on your opponent you will keep him off balance and create new openings.

Controlling the same side sleeve grip

Here are the basics of how to use the sleeve grip for any basic forward throw.

Grab the sleeve with your bottom three fingers leaving your thumb and forefinger relaxed (1). Pull the sleeve up and out past your ear (2), turn your head (3), and continue to pull forward twisting your pinky finger up (4).

Transitions to Ground Fighting

There are four ways to win in Judo: throwing, holding, choking and arm-locking. Therefore, 3 of the 4 ways to win are on the ground. Having a strong grappling base is essential to becoming a champion in Judo.

One of the biggest opportunities to attack is during the transition from standing throws and going to the ground. During this period, most fighters mentally relax for a split second, making it a perfect opportunity to use the surprise element.

It is important to practice this transition in order to sharpen your focus on ground techniques before you hit the ground. By concentrating on transition training, your mind and body will work together in competition for more scoring opportunities.

Ouchi Gari to Yoko Shio Gatame (big inside leg trip to side control)

From a same side stance (1), attack the leg trip (2 & 3). Immediately, push the leg through to pass (4 & 5). Once you have head control (6), start to walk your foot up the mat, then pull out your leg keeping it straight as possible (7) and once out, past your foot as far back as possible to stop your opponent from turning in (8). Switch hips and secure the hold (9).

Competitive Judo

167

Ko Uchi gari to Tate Shio Gatame (small inside leg trip to body mount)

From the same side stance (1), attack the leg trip (3 & 4). Immediately, control the knee (5), and gain control of the head (6). Once you have head control use your foot to pry out your other leg (7), and control the pin (8 & 9).

Competitive Judo

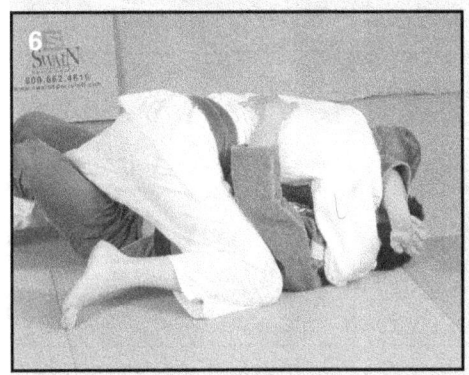

Tai Otoshi to Juji Gatame (side body drop to arm lock)

From a basic stance attack the throw (1, 2 & 3). Immediately, put your knee into opponent's side to control their body from turning (4), step over and pinch your knees together (5). Then, sit back making sure your backside is tight to his body (6), and apply an arm-lock making sure his pinky finger is pointing down (7).

Competitive Judo

Tai Otoshi to Kuzure Kesa Katame (side body drop to hold)

From a same side stance attack the throw (1, 2 & 3), immediately spin around opponent's head and place your knee against his chest to stop him from turning (4). Put your hand through and under their arm (5) as you lower your body to gain control of the arm for the pin (6).

O Soto Gari to Kesa Gatame (out side reap to hold)

From a basic same side stance attack the throw (1, 2 & 3), follow the opponent to the ground landing your body on top of his to secure the hold (4 & 5)

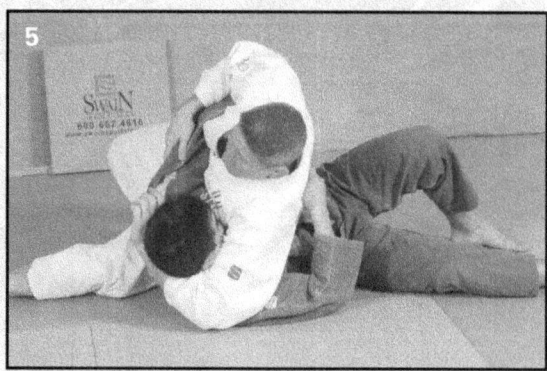

Competitive Judo

Tomoe Nage to Tate Shio Gatame (back sacrifice to hold)

From a basic stance (1), pull your opponent back diagonally to the back (2), and attack the throw (3). Make sure your foot is on the opponent's far hip (4). Then, extend your knee and pull down with the upper body grip (5) as the opponent lays flat (6), then roll back over to the hold (7).

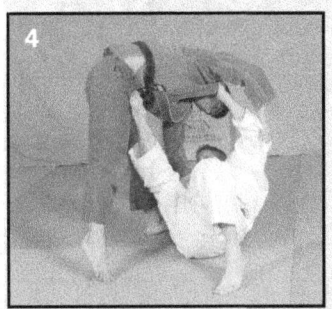
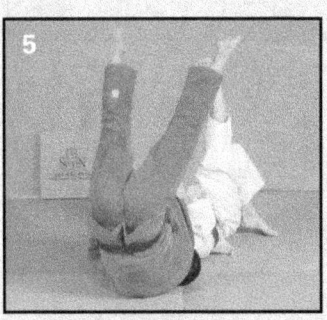
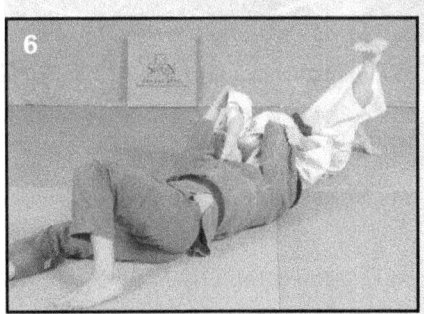

Championship Judo

Ko Soto Gari to Kazure Kami Shio Gatame (Leg trip to front hold)

From an opposite side grip (1), attack the throw (2 & 3) as the opponent goes down, control his upper body so he doesn't turn (4). Immediately, hook the elbow so he cannot turn away (5). Pull him back while your lower your hips to the ground for the pin (6).

Sumi Gaeshi to Yoko Shio Gatame (side roll to hold)

Start with an opposite side stance. Grab the sleeve and pull back (1). Step in with your left foot and sit straight back to roll the opponent over (2) to control the opponent's shoulder with your chin (3). Then, maintain the hold (4).

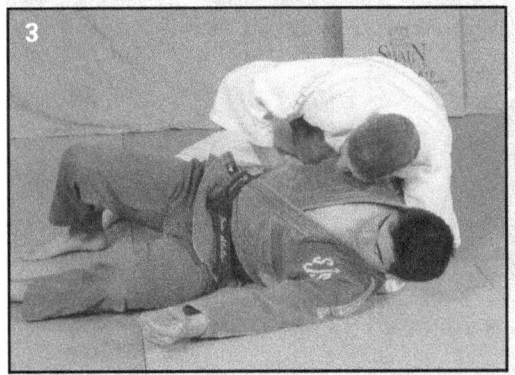
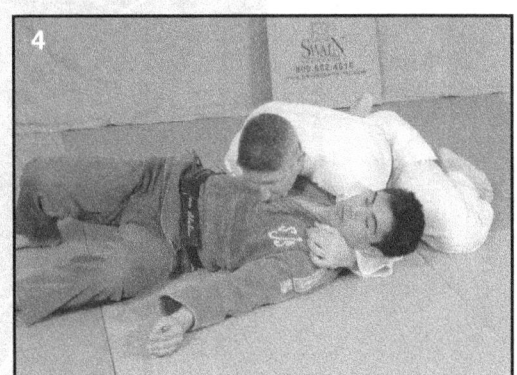

Taio Toshi to Waki Gatame (side body throw to arm lock)

From an opposite side grip (1), attack the throw (3 & 4). As the opponent turns to his stomach to avoid the throw (3), trap the wrist between your neck and shoulder (4), sit out and extend his arm for the lock (5).

Competitive Judo

Uchi Mata counter to Ude Garami (counter the inside leg throw to arm lock)

Opponent attacks the throw (1). Block with your hips (2), pull the sleeve hand in as he continues to attack (3). Then, ride the opponent to the ground (4), and maintain control moving up his body (5). Then, hook the arm (6), key lock the wrist with both hands (7), and move around the head pinching your knees to control his upper body (8). Rip the arm toward you first to break their grip (9). Then, back away close to the body to apply the arm-lock (10).

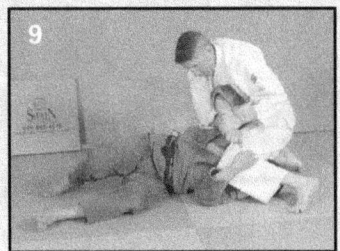

Championship Judo

Morote Gari counter to San Gaku Jime (double leg counter)

The opponent attacks a double leg takedown (1). Sprawl back and move you hips in (2,) then quickly jump into a triangle (3), grab the belt and roll to the side (4). Once on your side, first control the far arm by pulling it towards you (5 & 6), then control the closer arm with your wrist or key lock (7), and apply arm-lock (8) or triangle choke by squeezing your knees together (9). Another option is to come across for the hold (10).

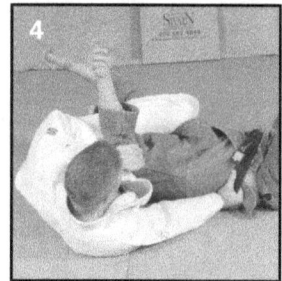

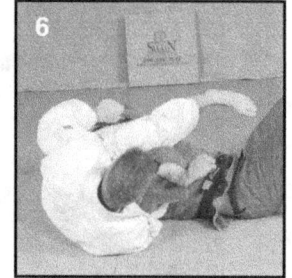
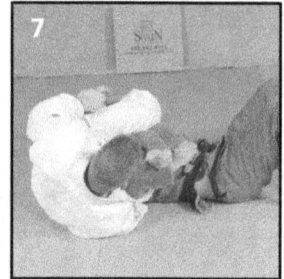

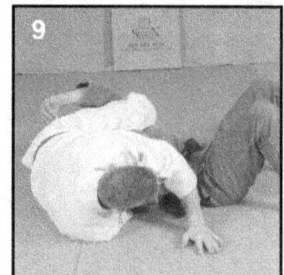

Competitive Judo

Ippon Seio counter to Juji Gatame (counter the hip throw to arm lock)

The opponent attacks with the hip throw (1). Block the action with hips (2), and enter with your lead foot and arm (3) maintaining his wrist control (4). Begin to pull the arm towards his head (5) until he lifts up so you can stick your leg under his head (6). Then, roll over and control the arm (7). Pull the arm towards his head (8 & 9) to finish the arm-lock (10).

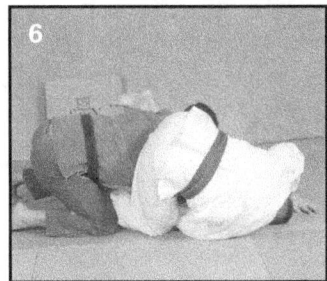

Chapter 5

Training Methods

Warm up and Partner Drills

1. FROG LEAP

Partner has legs apart and is bent over. Person jumps over and crawls between partner's legs.

2. JUMP OVER

Partner stays flat on the ground on his/her stomach or in the turtle position, and you jump keeping both legs together on the side over your partner.

 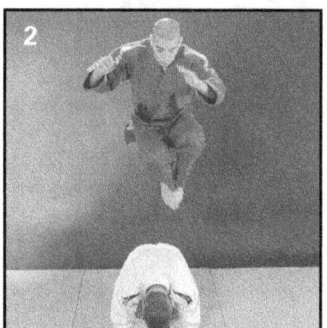 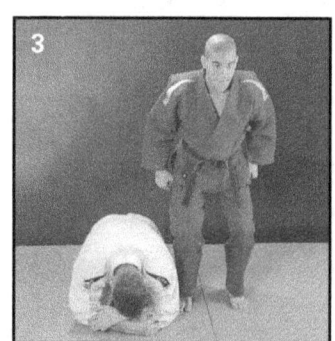

 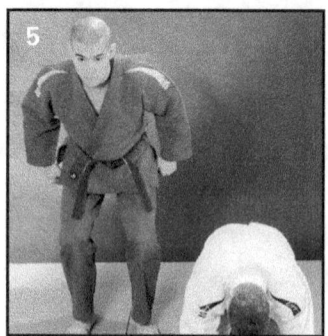

Training Methods

3. ELBOW SNAP

Partner is an arm length away facing you with arms open wide and hands facing inward. Hold your own lapel up high around your chest, and with legs apart twist upper body and snap with your elbow the partner's hand.

4. FRONT KICK

Partner is facing you with arms extended and his/her palms facing down. You kick across trying to touch the top of your foot to your partner's hand. Toes should be pointing down.

183

Championship Judo

5. KNEE TOUCH

Have partner face you with both hands hip high and palms facing down as you lift your knees straight up trying to touch partner's hands. It looks like a soldier marching.

6. LEG RAISE

Your partner should have legs apart, as you lay on your back with head facing partner's body. Hold the partner's ankle and raise legs straight towards partner's belt and push legs down. Do not let legs touch floor. You may also push to the sides.

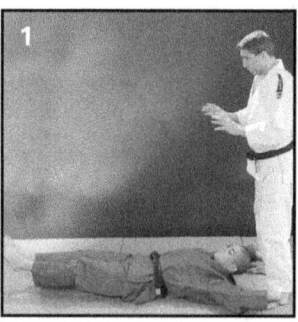  

 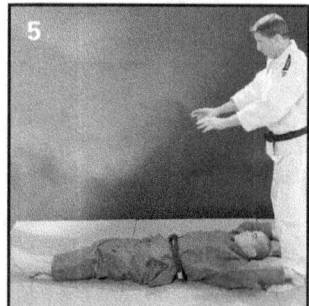

Training Methods

7. LEG PRESS

Lay on your back with your feet on your partner's chest that is facing you and putting his/her weight on your feet and legs. You should slowly bend your knees and bring partner close to you and push his/her weight back up. It is important that the partner keeps his/her back and legs straight like a board so the leg press is easier.

8. SIT UPS

Sit facing your partner and tangle or lock each other's legs and do sit-ups. Come up and down at the same time.

 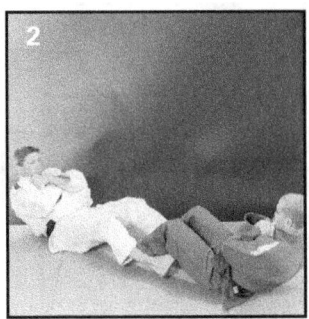 

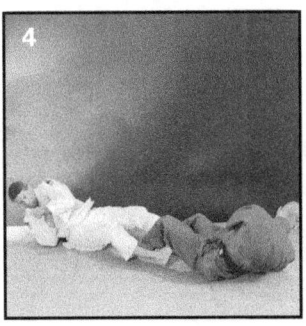 

9. FORWARD STRETCH

Face your partner with legs apart as far as you can with the soles of your feet touching the soles of your partner's feet. Hold your partner's hands and have him/her pull you forward as he/she pulls back and lies down on his/her back. It will stretch your legs. Reverse and pull your partner forward.

Training Methods

10. FORWARD STRETCH STANDING

Both you and your partner face each other with legs wide apart. Hold each other's shoulders and push forward and down without bending knees.

11. SIDE STRETCH STANDING

With legs apart, stand side to side with your partner. Hold each other's hands that are next to each other down low. Hold the outer hands up above your heads. The partner should pull your upper arm over his/her head and you should feel your side stretching.

Championship Judo

12. BACK TO BACK STRETCH

Stand with your back to your partner's back, knees bent and elbows locked together. Bend forward pulling your partner onto your back. Your partner should relax and stretch his/her back. Reverse positions.

13. CHICKEN FIGHT

You and your partner each squat and face each other while holding on to your own lapel around your chest area. While still squatting, do quick jumps towards each other to off balance the other. You lose if your knees or butt touches the mat.

Training Methods

14. TWIST AND OFF BALANCE

You and your partner face each other in a kneeling position, upper body straight. Hold onto your partner's uniform and try to off balance each other by twisting and try to get your partner's back on the ground.

 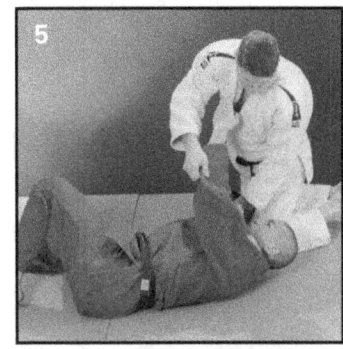

15. SUMO

Face each other with legs wide enough apart so that both of your hands stay on the ground. Try to push your partner straight back to a wall. No twisting is allowed due to safety, especially in limited space.

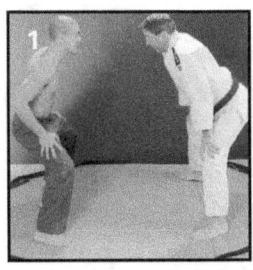   

Championship Judo

16. TUG OF WAR

Start in the middle of the room holding your partner's hands crossed over or your partner's sleeves and pull all the way to your side of the wall.

17. STANDING ARM WRESTLE

Have legs apart with one leg forward and one leg back hold hand like in the arm wrestle style and using your whole body try to off balance your partner. If you move your foot you lose.

Training Methods

18. STAND UP BACK TO BACK

Sit down with your back to your partner's back. Use only your legs and each other's back as a support to get up and sit down.

Basic 12-Week Judo Program

The basic 12-week judo program is designed for two, 1-hour classes each week. The first two weeks should concentrate heavily on drills and falling techniques. Grappling techniques will be introduced first because both partners are on the ground in a more controlled and safe environment. Throwing techniques will be introduced toward the latter half of the course after the students have become familiar with the falling and drills. It is advised not to teach submission techniques, such as chokes and armlocks, unless students are at least 13 years old. However, this is up to the school owner's discretion. The outline is arranged for you to chose from a selection of warm-ups and partner drills in order to keep the class changing and interesting.

All classes should include the following core instruction below:

Bow in

10 min Warm-up / Partner Drills

10 min Falling Techniques

10 min Grappling Standing Drills

15 min Technique Teaching

10 min *Live training (2 min x 4 rounds with 30 sec. in between rounds)*option

05 min Warm-down + (stretching)

Bow out

First Month
Week One Class 1

Bow in

Explain history and philosophy of Judo

Warm-up

Falling techniques

Forward roll

Grappling drills

Grappling hold (Basic Kesa gatame)

Bow out

Training Methods

Week One Class 2
- Bow in
- Warm-up
- Falling techniques/rolls
- Grappling drills
- Variations to cross chest hold (Kesa gatame)
- Escape Kesa Gatame
- Live Drill (escape hold 25 seconds) x 2
- Bow out

Week Two Class 3
- Bow in
- Warm-up
- Falling techniques
- Grappling drills
- Grappling hold shoulder hold (Kami shio Gatame)
- Escape
- Live Drill (escape 25 seconds) x2
- Bow out

Week Two Class 4
- Bow in
- Warm-up
- Partner drills
- Falling techniques
- Grappling hold—four corners hold (Tate shio Gatame)
- Escape
- Live Drill (escape 25 seconds) x 2
- Bow out

Week Three Class 5
- Bow in
- Warm-up
- Falling techniques
- Grappling positions/gripping
- Grappling hold

Escape
Live drill (escape 25 seconds) x 2
Bow out

Week Three Class 6
Bow in
Warm-up
Falling techniques
Grappling turnovers (2)
Grappling hold, four corners hold (Tate shio Gatame)
Escape
Live Drill (escape 25 seconds)
Bow out

Week Four Class 7
Bow in
Warm-up
Falling techniques
Grappling drills/turnovers
Grappling hold, four corners hold (Tate shio Gatame)
Escape
Live Drill (escape 25 seconds) x 2
Bow out

Week Four Class 8
Bow in
Warm-up
Falling Techniques
Grappling drills/turnovers—review
Grappling hold, all holds review
Escape—all holds review
Test for Falling and Grappling (Patch for "Falling" and patch for "Grappling" holding Techniques)
Bow out

Second Month

Week Five Class 9
- Bow in
- Warm-up
- Falling techniques
- Standing partner drills
- Gripping—explanation
- Stance and Body Movement—explanation
- Off Balancing—explanation
- Push Pull Theory—explanation
- Live Drill—practice all above with partner
- Bow out

Week Five Class 10
- Bow in
- Warm-up
- Falling techniques
- Standing partner drills
- Off Balancing—Review
- Throwing technique #1—knee wheel (Hiza garuma)
- Drill—knee wheel with partner on knees then standing
- Live drills—3 sets of 10 throws each
- Bow out

Week Six Class 11
- Bow in
- Warm-up
- Falling techniques
- Standing partner drills
- Throwing Technique Review #1 forward direction—knee wheel (Hiza garuma)
- Drill—knee wheel with partner on knees then standing
- Introduce counter to throw
- Drill counter to throw
- Live drills—10 throws each/10 counters each
- Bow out

Week Six Class 12
- Bow in
- Warm-up
- Falling techniques
- Standing partner drills
- Throwing technique—#2 hip throw (O Goshi)
- Live drills—3 sets of 10 throws each
- Bow out

Week Seven Class 13
- Bow in
- Warm-up
- Falling techniques
- Standing partner drills
- Throwing technique—review #2 hip throw (Ogoshi)
- Introduce counter to throw
- Live drills—3 sets of 10 counter throws each
- Bow out

Week Seven Class 14
- Bow in
- Warm-up
- Falling techniques
- Partner drills
- Throwing technique #3 rear direction—reaping leg (Osoto gari)
- Live drills—3 sets of 10 throws
- Bow out

Week Eight Class 15
- Bow in
- Warm-up
- Falling techniques
- Partner drills
- Throwing technique #3 rear direction—reaping leg (Osoto gari)
- Introduce counter to #3

Training Methods

> Live drills—3 sets of 10 counter throws
> Bow out
>
> **Week Eight Class 16**
> Bow in
> Warm-up
> Falling techniques
> Partner drills
> Review throwing fundamentals
> Throwing technique—review all throws
> Review all counters
> Test for throwing and counters (Patch for throwing and counter techniques)
> Bow out
>
> ## Third Month
> **Week Nine Class 17**
> Bow in
> Warm-up
> Falling techniques
> Partner drills
> Grappling drills
> Technique—pass the legs
> Live back to back drill
> Bow out
>
> **Week Nine Class 18**
> Bow in
> Warm-up
> Falling techniques
> Partner drills
> Grappling drills
> Armlocks fundamentals and safety
> Technique—armlock #1 entangles arm lock (ude Garame)
> variations of #1
> Live back to back drill
> Bow out

Week Ten Class 19
- Bow in
- Warm-up
- Falling techniques
- Partner drills
- Grappling drills
- Technique—armlock #2 cross body lock (Juji Gatame) variations of #2
- Live back to back drill
- Bow out

Week Ten Class 20
- Bow in
- Warm-up
- Falling techniques
- Partner drills
- Grappling drills
- Technique—armlock review #1 and #2
- Release armlock—review
- Live back to back drill
- Bow out

Week Eleven Class 21
- Bow in
- Warm-up
- Falling techniques
- Partner drills
- Grappling drills
- Choking fundamental and safety
- Technique—choking #1 cross lock choke (Gyaku-Juji-jime)
- Variations to #1
- Technique—Choking #2 half cross choke
- Live back to back drill
- Bow out

Training Methods

Week Eleven Class 22
    Bow in
    Warm-up
    Falling techniques
    Partner drills
    Grappling drills
    Technique—Choking #3 naked arm choke (Hadaka-Jime)
    Variations to #3
    Live back to back drill
    Bow out

Week Twelve Class 23
    Bow in
    Warm-up
    Falling techniques
    Partner drills
    Grappling drills
    Technique—Choking #4 single wing choke (Kata ha Jime)
    Test all choking techniques (patch for choking techniques)
    Bow out

Week Twelve Class 24
    Bow in
    Warm-up
    Falling Techniques
    Partner Drills
    Grappling Drills
    Technique—Review all standing and ground
    Test for complete Level One training course (patch for level one course)
    Bow out

Judo Band Training

The judo band provides dynamic resistance exercises. They come in a range of resistance levels indicated by color coding. The appropriated color should be selected according to the athlete's ability to perform the exercises through correct range of motion at the given sets and repetitions. The judo band can be used both for single plane exercises, such as the biceps curls, and multi-planes functional exercises, such as the kata guruma pulls.

Depending on the specific activity, the judo band can be utilized at the dojo or at home. It is portable, light, and easy to attach to different objects, such as door handles, trees, fences, your own body, and many other options. Most of the following judo band exercises are demonstrated with BOB.

Exercises that mimic specific judo movement patterns allow strength gains in the functional motions. The following program also provides a few rehabilitation exercises for the injured judoka. Those exercises can be completed during the practice time at the dojo and may increase the injured athlete's feeling of still being part of the team. In addition, the injured athlete can also use the judo band to perform variety of judo techniques in a controlled environment. The judo specific exercises are also excellent for the beginning judoka, who can learn the motor pathways before even using an opponent.

The judo band program can be used as a separate unit of practice or as part of a warm up.

Judo Band Exercises
Scapular retraction
Stand facing BOB. Hold the judo band with your arm straight in front of your body and parallel to the floor. Squeeze your shoulder blades towards each other while keeping your arms straight.

Internal rotation in 45°
Stand with one side toward BOB. Hold the judo band with the hand closest to BOB. With your elbow flexed at 90°, internally rotate the arm. Make sure that you keep the elbow tight to the body through the range of motion.

External rotation in 45°
Stand with one side toward BOB. Hold the judo band with the hand that is away from BOB. While your elbow is flexed at 90°, externally rotate the arm. Make sure that you keep the elbow tight next to the body through the range of motion.

Internal rotation in 90°
Stand with your back to BOB. Hold the judo band with the arm laterally raised to 90°, the elbow flexed at 90°, and your shoulder externally rotated (the palm of the hand should face the ceiling). Internally rotate your arm without displacing the shoulder forward.

External rotation in 90°

Stand facing BOB Hold the judo band with the arm laterally raised at 90°, elbow flexed to 90°, and the shoulder internally rotated (the palm of the hand should face the floor). Externally rotate the shoulder without displacing the shoulder backward.

Serratus punches

Stand with your back to BOB. Hold the judo band with forward raised arm and straight elbow. Punch forward while keeping the elbow straight.

Ankle Inversion

Sit down on the mat with your legs straight and crossed just above the ankle. Wrap the judo band around your feet. Move the upper foot as if you are trying to see the ball of it.

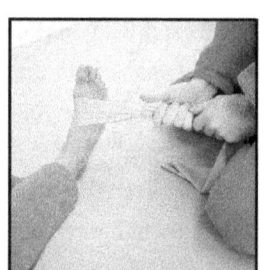

Ankle eversion

Sit down on the mat with your legs straight. Wrap the judo band around your feet. Rotate the ankle as if you are trying to bring the pinky toward the shin.

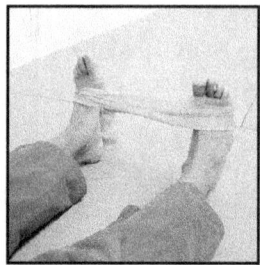 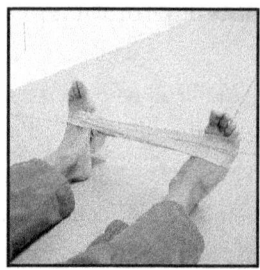

Training Methods

Ankle plantar flexion

Sit down with your legs straight on the floor. Wrap the judo band around one foot just below the toes, and hold the edges of the judo band with your hand in order to keep the tension. Point your ankle and toes.

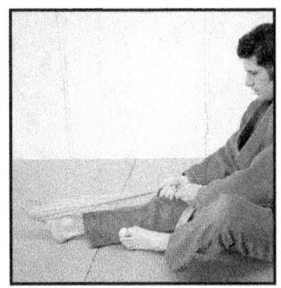

Ankle dorsi flexion

Sit down on the mat with your legs straight with one leg on top of the other. Wrap the judo band around the feet and move the ankle of the upper leg towards you.

Diagonal 1

Stand with one side toward BOB. Hold the judo band with the hand closest to BOB, with a straight arm beside the body. Perform a movement as if you are going to take an apple out of your pocket and throw it behind the opposite ear.

Championship Judo

Diagonal 2

Stand with one side toward BOB. Hold the judo band with the arm away from BOB, and the arm crossed to the opposite waist line. Perform a movement as if you pulled out a sword out of its scabbard.

Scaption thumb up

Stand with your back to BOB. Hold the judo band with your arm straight and close to your body. Raise the arm in the scapular plane (just between front raises and lateral raises) with the thumb pointing up.

Scaption thumb down

The same movement as scaption thumb up, but with the thumb pointing down.

Straight arm raise

Stand either facing or with your back to BOB. Hold the judo band with the arm straight beside the body. Forward raise the arm to 90° while keeping a straight arm.

Training Methods

Lateral arm raise

Stand with your side facing BOB. Hold the judo band with the arm away from BOB. Raise the arm sideways to 90°.

Upward rows

Stand facing BOB. Hold the judo band with both hands down straight and close to each other. Make an upward pull, raising the arm to the side with flexed elbows. The elbows should point sideways and the wrist should point toward the face.

Standing rows

Stand facing BOB. Hold the judo band with the arms straight and forward raised. Pull the judo band beside the body in the nipple line, while flexing the elbows.

Shoulder Shrug

Stand up straight with the judo band wrapped around your feet and your hands holding the judo band straight beside the body. Lift your shoulder as if you are trying to touch your ears, while keeping the arms straight beside the body.

Championship Judo

Overhead elbow extensions
Kneel down with your back facing BOB. Hold the judo band with your elbow flexed overhead. Extend the elbows while avoiding any movement in the shoulders.

Triceps pull downs
Stand facing BOB. Hold the judo band with your elbows flexed and tight to the sides of your body. Extend your elbows down, keeping tight to the body and avoiding any shoulder movement.

Biceps curls
Stand straight and wrap the judo band around your feet. Hold the judo band with your arms straight beside your body and the palm of your hands facing forward. Flex your elbows to their full range of motion and keep the elbows tight to your body, avoiding any movement in the shoulders.

Wrist flexion
Sit on a chair with your elbows flexed on the legs. Wrap the judo band around your feet and hold it with your hands facing the ceiling and the wrists hanging outside the knees. Curl the wrists.

Training Methods

Wrist extension

Sit the same way as in the wrist flexion, but this time the wrists should be facing the floor. Extend the wrists.

Wrist ulnar deviation

Stand facing BOB. Hold the judo band with straight arms beside the body. Wrists should be in a neutral position (as in a military stance). Pull the wrist backward to the side of the pinky finger.

Wrist radial deviation

Stand with your back facing BOB. Hold the |judo band in the same position as in the ulnar deviation exercise. Pull the wrist forward to the side of the thumb.

Wrist pronation

Stand with your side facing BOB. Hold the judo band with the arm closest to BOB. The elbow should be flexed to 90° and tight to the trunk; palm facing up.

Rotate the wrist so the palm will face your body.

Wrist supination

Stand with your side facing BOB. Hold the judo band with the arm away from BOB. The elbow should be flexed to 90° and tight to the trunk; palm facing down. Rotate the wrist so the palm will face up.

Squat facing BOB

Stand facing BOB. Wrap the judo band around your waist, feet shoulder width apart. Flex the knees to 90° and then fully extend them. Keep your back straight throughout the movement.

Squat back to BOB

The same movement as squat facing BOB, but stand with your back to BOB.

Resistive forward lunge

Stand facing BOB. Wrap the judo band around your waist. Keep your hands on your hips. The working leg is placed forward and the uninvolved leg backward. Bend the knees. The back knee should almost touch the mat and the front knee should not pass the great toe line. Extend back the knees and the hips. Keep your back straight throughout the movement.

Training Methods

Assisted forward lunge

Stand with your back facing BOB and wrap the judo band around your waist. Perform the same movement as the resistive forward lunge.

Resistive lateral squat

Stand with your side facing BOB and wrap the judo band around your waist, with your feet shoulder width apart. Step sideways toward BOB and squat to 90°. Extend your knees as you step back to the beginning position (stepping with the leg closer to BOB).

Assisted lateral squat

This is basically the same movement as the resistive lateral squat exercise, except this time you should step sideways with the leg that is away from BOB.

Kuzushi wrists

Hold the judo band in each hand with thumbs pointing up. Secure the band with your last three fingers, leaving your thumb and forefinger relaxed. Flex your wrists straight back and bend your knees slightly at the same time. This motion jerks your opponent off balance.

Championship Judo

Sleeve arm pull
Start by gripping both bands in one hand with wrist flexed back. Pull past your head and turn your pinky up. This simulates your pulling sleeve arm.

Ippon seo nage
Start by gripping both bands in one hand with wrist flexed back. Pull with the sleeve arm and step in with the opposite foot placing the band in your elbow crease. Step back with other foot and squat, keeping your back straight.

Te o toshi one sleeve
Grab both bands to simulate the sleeve of a uniform. Pull turning pinky up. Bring your other hand across to catch the two bands as your feet and body turn 180 degrees. Continue pulling the bands until your arm is extended.

Training Methods

Kata Guruma

Grab both bands to simulate the sleeve of a uniform. Pull to you while turning your pinky up and keeping your elbow up. Lower your body and step in and across BOB. Then left and turn for the finish.

Kuzushi elbow — *off balance position of elbow and pulling hand*

This is important on all throws. In order to off balance your opponent, your elbow must stay up with pinky turned up as you pull your opponent into you for the throw.

Lapel arm kuzushi — *off balance motion of lapel hand*

This motion imitates the movement of your hand that is grabbing the opponent's lapel. Simply bring your elbow up with your hand to your ear.

Uchi Mata — *inner thigh throw*

This motion imitates the pull of this particular throw. Use the basic movements of the lapel and sleeve grip we have discussed. The key is to pull first then step in and around. Turn your head to look away from Bob as you extend your pull.

12-Week Judo Band Training Program

Weeks 1-3 Injury Prevention

Day 1
    Scapular retraction
    Internal rotation in 45°
    External rotation in 45°
    Serratus punches
    Ankle inversion
    Ankle eversion
    Scaption thumb down

Day 2
    Diagonal 1
    Diagonal 2
    Internal rotation in 90°
    External rotation in 90°
    Scaption thumb up
    Ankle plantar flexion
    Ankle dorsi flexion

3 sets of 15 reps with 30 sec rest intervals (RI).

Weeks 4-7 Total Body Toning

Day 1
    Straight arm rise
    Squat facing Bob
    Upward rows
    Resistive forward lunge
    Overhead elbow extensions
    Lateral lunge
    Wrist flexion
    Wrist extension
    Triceps pull down

Training Methods

Day 2
- Standing rows
- Assistive forward lunge
- Shoulder shrug
- Lateral lunge
- Biceps curls
- Squat back to Bob
- Lateral arm rise
- Wrist ulnar deviation
- Wrist radial deviation

Week 4—12 reps x 4 sets of light judo band, 30 sec RI
Week 5—10 reps x 4 sets of medium judo band, 45 sec RI
Week 6—8 reps x 3 sets of strong judo band, 60 sec RI
Week 7—8 reps x 4 sets of strong judo band, 90 sec RI

- Change the order of the exercises each week, but make sure that your sequence gives enough time to each muscle group to recover. For example, do not give squats after lunges, instead give shoulder or other upper body exercise.

Weeks 8-10 Judo Specific Exercises
Day 1
- Kuzushi-wrists
- Sleeve arm pulls
- Te o toshi
- Ippon seo nage
- Shoulder shrug
- Wrist pronation

Day 2
- Kuzushi—elbow
- Lapel arm
- Te o toshi on one sleeve
- Kata guruma
- Standing row
- Wrist supination

Week 8—12 repsx 2 sets each side, light judo band.
Week 9—10 repsx 2 sets each side, medium judo band.
Week 10—8 repsx 2 sets each side, strong judo band.

- RI of 60 sec in all weeks
- Emphasis in this phase should be on accurate form!

Weeks 11-12 Judo Speed Exercises
Day 1
  Uchi mata pulls
  Ippon seo nage
  Te o toshi on one sleeve
  Kata guruma pulls
  Te o toshi

Day 2
  Te o toshi
  Kata guruma
  Uchi mata pulls
  Sleeve arm pulls
  Ippon seo nage

  Week 11—3 sets, 45 sec, 30 sec, 20 sec.
  Week 12—3 sets, 30 sec, 20 sec, 10 sec

- RI should be in 1:4 ration e.g. after 10 second set a 40 second RI should be given.

Emphasis in this phase should be on maximum (amount of reps) in the given time.

Training Methods

Body Weight Exercises with a Partner

Functional body weight exercises for judo requires no equipment but the bodyweight of you and your opponent. The variety of exercises provided in this program emphasizes the lower extremities, upper extremities, and the trunk. A progression can be achieved by increasing the amount of body weight used in an exercise (choosing a heavier opponent), increasing the duration of the exercise, or increasing the number of repetition or sets.

The following body weight exercises train the sensory and the motor pathways specifically for judo. Whereas in weight lifting the lifted weight is distributed equally (symmetrically) throughout the body, in body weight exercises with a partner, the person learns how to work with human bodies where weight is not distributed equally, just like in judo. In addition, in the following exercises both people work at the same time. While one is performing the movement, the other one usually requires stabilizing the body in order to support the partner.

The human body is the most sophisticated training instrument. It has 700 muscles and 206 bones, and it automatically adjusts to increase in resistance levels.

Sit-ups with legs around the partner

One partner stands with slightly bent knees and tightened abs. Sitting person wraps the legs around the standing person's waist and performs a full range motion sit-up.

Sit-ups while partner is in 6 contact points position

While the partner is in 6 points contact position, hook your feet between his/her thighs and sit on his/her upper back. As you extend the trunk, the partner should flex the neck (bring the chin toward the chest). Then flex the trunk to perform a sit-up, while the partner extends the neck.

One partner sit-ups, other partner straight leg raises

Both people lie on their backs. One person with bent knees (feet on the ground) and the other holds the partner's legs above his/her head. The person who holds the legs flexes the hips to 90° keeping knees straight and the other person performs a regular sit-up.

 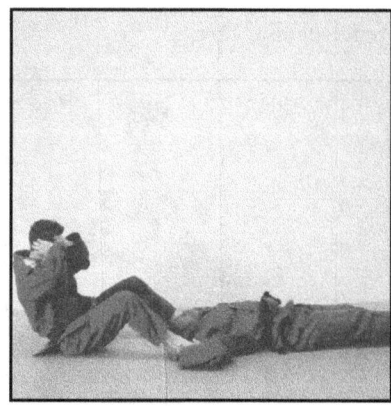

Training Methods

Sit-ups with squeezing fist into the abs

Lie down on your back with bent knees and feet on the floor. Your partner should kneel beside you and stick a fist just above your naval as you perform a sit-up. Make sure to keep the abdominal muscles tight throughout the motion in order to prevent pain.

 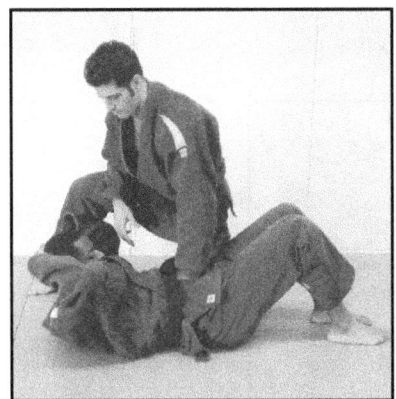

Trunk extension with leg around the partner

One person stands with a straight back and slightly bent knees. The other person should be in a prone position with legs wrapped around the standing person's waist. Perform a trunk extension. Do not hyperextend the back.

Seated rows

Sit in front of each other in a comfortable split position. Grab each other's hands so one will have both hands on top and the other will have both hands on the bottom. Perform straight pulls while the other person slightly resists the movement. Follow with your partner pulling while you resist the pull. Alter the gripping, have the bottom grip, or have one hand grip on top and the other on the bottom.

 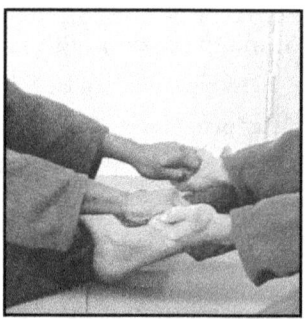

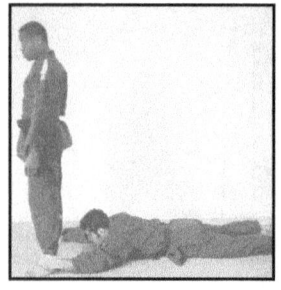 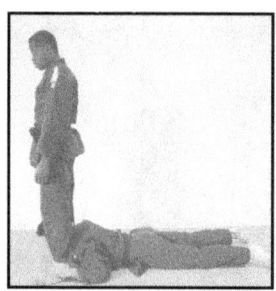

Chin up while holding partner's legs

Lie down on your stomach while holding your partner's ankles with straight arms. As your partner stands still, pull with your arms so your head will be between your partner's legs. Then the partner steps forward and you repeat the movement.

Training Methods

Mat pulls while holding partner's sleeves

Stand up with knees bent and hold your partner's sleeves as he/she lies on his/her back between your legs. As you extend your knees, forcefully pull your partner's sleeves so their head will be between your legs. Step back and perform the movement again. Your partner should maintain his/her feet off the mat.

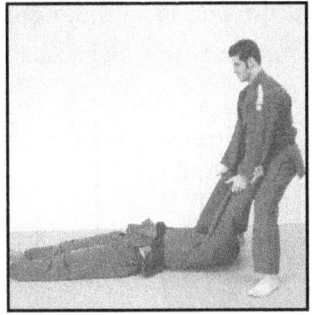 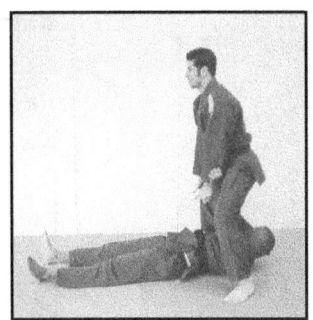

Side by side pulls

Sit by each other and grab each other's right hand if sitting left to left or left hand if sitting right to right. Pull toward you while rotating the wrist so the palm of the hand will face the ceiling. You can add rotation to the trunk for core work.

 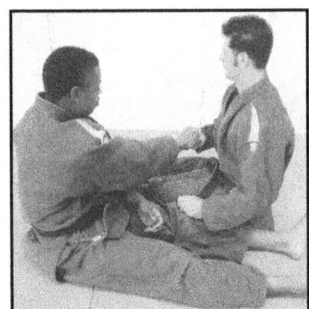 

Kata Guruma proper lifting form

Championship Judo

Kata Guruma carry with lunges

Pick up your partner with kata guruma and perform a traditional forward lunge.

Kata Guruma carry with trunk twist

Pick up your partner with kata guruma and perform left and right trunk twist.

Kata Guruma lunges with twist

Pick up your partner with kata guruma and perform a traditional forward lunge. As you lunge twist the trunk to the side of the forward leg.

Training Methods

Kata Guruma carry squats

Pick up your partner with kata guruma and perform a squat.

Running Kata Guruma carry

Pick up the partner with kata guruma and run for the given distance.

Hand shake push-up

Have both partners in push-up position in front of each other. Shake each other's hands and alternate to the other hand.

Wheelbarrow

Lie on your stomach while your partner stands and holds your ankles at waist level. Extend your elbows and approach forward with one arm following the other. Make sure to keep your legs, torso, and neck in one line!

Japanese Wheelbarrow

Lie on your stomach while your partner stands and holds your ankles at waist level. Extend your elbows and approach forward alternating arms with one forearm touching the mat. Make sure to keep your legs, torso, and neck in one line!

Training Methods

Wheelbarrow push-up

Lie on your stomach while your partner stands and holds your ankles at waist level. Extend your elbows and approach forward with one arm following the other. After two steps perform a push-up. Be certain you keep your legs, torso, and neck in one line!

Ura Nage/suplex drill

Your partner should be in 6 contact points position as you hold your arm around him. Interlock your fingers or hold the other hand at the wrist. With flexed hips and knees and maintaining a flat or slightly arched back, extend the knees and the hips and lift your partner off the ground. In the following repetition, the partner should stay off the ground.

Rock & roll drill

Hold your partner's right sleeve with your left hand and your left arm should be wrapped around his or her waist (o goshi grip). Lift your partner so his body will be in front of you as in carrying a baby. Then lift your partner and bring your hips in so your partner will be lying on your back. Repeat the movement.

Supine hamstring curls, partner tries to pin

Lie down on your back with your legs straight and your arms holding your partner's shoulders. Your partner is in a bear position facing your legs on top of you. Simultaneously, bend your knees as the feet stay stationary on the mat and push your partner away with your arms. As you move forward, your partner should close the gap and try to stay on top of you. Make sure that your back stays flat on the mat.

Three people pulls while holding the belt

Lie on your back with straight legs and hold your partners' belts as they stand beside you and facing each other. Pull with your arms to lift your body off the mat as your feet stay in contact with it. Your legs, torso, and head should be in one line.

Pushing partner at the chest forward

Stand in front of your partner with right leg slightly forward. Push your partner forward and step forward with the leading leg (right leg). Your partner should give a 50% resistance to assure smooth and rhythmic movement. Repeat with the opposite leg leading.

Training Methods

Resisting a sideways push

Stand with your side to your partner. Your partner should push you at shoulder level and you should give him or her a 50% resistance in order to assure smooth and rhythmic movement.

Holding partners belt forward run

Stand with your back facing your partner. As your partner holds the back of your belt, try to run as fast as you can to the given point. Your partner should give a 50% resistance in order to assure smooth and rhythmic movement.

Holding partners belt backward run

Stand facing your partner. As your partner holds the front of your belt, try to run backward as fast as you can. Your partner should give a 50% resistance in order to assure smooth and rhythmic movement.

Piggy bag runs

Baby carry runs

Hold your partner as if you are carrying a baby. Your partner can assist by wrapping her/his arm around your neck. Run to a given point.

Bear runs while partner hangs on belt

Get into a bear position (on your hands and knees, with your butt up in the top of the triangle). As your partner's lying on his or her back (head pointing toward your head) and holding on to the front of your belt, move forward as fast as you can, carrying the partner.

12-Week Body Weight Exercises with a Partner Program

Weeks 1-2 Muscular Endurance Training

Day 1
- Sit-ups with legs around partner
- Seated rows
- Kata guruma carry with lunges
- Wheel barrel
- Chin-ups while holding partner's legs

Day 2
- Sit-ups with partner in 4 position
- Sitting pulls side by side
- Kata guruma carry with trunk twist
- Japanese wheel barrel
- Kata guruma carry squats

Week 1—Perform 3 sets of 20 repetitions with 30 seconds rest intervals (RI).
Week 2—Perform 3 sets of 15 reps with 20 seconds RI.

Weeks 3-6 Muscle Growth (Hypertrophy)

Day 1
- Ura nage drill
- One partner sit-ups, other SLR
- Mat pulls while holding partner's sleeves
- Supine hamstring curls, other tries to pin
- Hand shake push ups

Day 2
- Trunk extensions with legs around partner
- Sit-ups with squeezing fist into the abs
- 3 people pulls while holding belts
- Squats
- Wheel barrel push-ups

Week 3—3 sets of 12 reps with 30 sec RI
Week 4—4 sets of 8 reps with 45 sec RI
Week 5—4 sets of 10 reps with 45 sec RI
Week 6—5 sets of 8 reps with 60 sec RI

Weeks 7-10 Strength Training
Day 1
> Rock & Roll drill
> Squat
> Hand shake pulls
> Ura nage drill

Day 2
> Trunk extensions/legs around partner
> Kata guruma lunges with a twist
> Mat pulls while holding partner's sleeves
> Sit ups/ legs wrapped on partner

In this phase the partner should be heavier than the opponent.
Week 7— 2 sets of 6 reps
Week 8—3 sets of 5 reps
Week 9—4 sets of 4 reps
Week 10—5 sets of 3 reps
RI should be 2-5 minutes.

Weeks 11-12 Strength Speed Training
Day 1
> Running kata guruma carry
> Resisting a sideways push
> Holding partner's belt-running backward
> Piggy bag runs

Training Methods

Day 2
- Pushing partner at the chest forward
- Holding partner's belt-running forward
- Baby carry runs
- Bear runs while partner hangs on belt

The distance length of these exercises should not exceed 50 meters. The exercises should be performed at maximum speed. Therefore, a minimum 3 minutes RI's should be given. Each exercise should compromise 3–5 repetitions.

Judo Terminology

Dojo: *Place of practice*
Hajime: *Begin*
Ippon: *Point*
Judo: *The gentle way*
Judo Gi: *Judo uniform*
Judoka: *Someone who does judo*
Ju-jitsu: *The variety of unarmed combat techniques from which judo derives*
Kodakan: *Headquarters of judo*
Kuzushi: *Off balancing*
Matte: *Wait*
Ne-waza: *Groundwork techniques*
Obi: *Belt*
Randori: *Free exercise*
Rei: *Bow*
Sensei: *Teacher*
Shiai: *Contest*
Sono-mama: *Freeze*
Sore-made: *Finish*
Tachi-waza: *Standing technique*
Tatami: *Judo mats*
Tori: *Person who does the throwing*
Uchi-komi: *Repetition practice of techniques*
Uke: *Person who is thrown*
Ukemi: *method of falling*
Waza: *Technique*
Wazari: *Half point*

NE-WAZA

Eri: *Collar or lapel of jacket*

Gatame: *Hold*

Juji: *Cross*

Juji-gatame: *Cross hold*

Kami: *Upper*

Kami-shiho-gatame: *Upper four quarters hold*

Kesa: *Oblique*

Kesa-gatame: *Oblique hold*

Okuri-eri-jime: *Sliding strangle*

Shiho: *Four Corners*

Shime: *Choke*

Tate: *Parallel*

Tate-shiho-gatame: *Astride four quarters hold*

Yoko: *Side*

Yoko-shiho-gatame: *Side four quarters hold*

TACHI-WAZA

Ashi: *Leg or foot*

Ashi-harai: *Foot sweep*

Gari: *Reap*

Guruma: *Wheel*

Harai: *Sweeping action*

Harai-goshi: *Sweeping hip throw*

Ippon-seoi-nage: *One arm*

Kata: *Shoulder; single or one of a pair*

Kata-guruma: *Shoulder wheel*
Ko: *Small*
Kosoto-gake: *Minor outer hook*
Kouchi-gari: *Minor inner reap*
Mata: *Thigh*
Morote-seoi-nage: *Two-handed shoulder throw*
O: *Large*
O-guruma: *Major wheel throw*
Osoto-gari: *Major outer reap*
Osoto-guruma: *Major outer wheel throw*
Ouchi-gari: *Major inner reap*
Seoi-nage: *Shoulder throw*
Soto: *Outside*
Tai: *Body*
Tai-otoshi: *Body drop*
Tomoe-nage: *Whirling or stomach throw*
Uchi: *Inside*
Uchimata: *Inner thigh*

About the Author

Mike Swain, a business marketing graduate from San Jose State University, is currently the president and CEO of Swain Sports International.

The name Mike Swain has become synonymous with judo world-wide. Swain made history in 1987 by becoming the first male World Champion from the western hemisphere. In addition, Mike has won or medaled in all major international tournaments including the Olympics (1988 bronze), World Championships (1985 silver , 1987 gold, 1989 silver), and Pan American Games (1987 gold). He is a four-time Olympian, five-time World Team member and was the 1996 US Olympic judo coach for the Atlanta Games.

To hone his skills during his competition career, Mike frequently traveled to Japan where he trained relentlessly for several hours a day. While in Japan, he chose to train at Nihon University, which is one of Japan's top Judo Universities, as well as with the Tokyo Police Academy.

In addition to his many awards, in 1985 Mike was honored as Black Belt Magazine's "Competitor of the Year" and in 1995 as "Instructor of the Year." Recently Mike received the prestigious "Titan Award" from the United States Olympic Committee as the pioneer for USA Judo. Other Titan recipients include Evander Holyfield for boxing and Dan Gable for wrestling.

Mike's wife Chie represented Brazil in the 1992 Olympic Games, and his father-in-law Chiaki Ishii won the bronze medal for Brazil in the 1972 Olympics. The Swain's have two children, daughter Sophia and son Masato.

Mike was also Co-producer of several martial art TV shows: Pro Judo, Pro Tae Kwon Do, and Sumo, which have all premiered on ESPN or ESPN2. In demand as a teacher, coach and seminar leader, Swain is also involved in market development for Century Martial Arts.

Honors and Awards

US World and Olympic Honors

1980	Moscow, Russia	Olympic Team Member
1984	Los Angeles, USA	Olympic Team Member
1988	Seoul, Korea	Olympic Team Captain
1992	Barcelona, Spain	Olympic Team Member
1996	Atlanta, USA	Men's Olympic Judo Coach
1977	Barcelona, Spain	World Team Member
1983	Moscow, Russia	World Team Member
1985	Seoul, Korea	World Team Member
1987	Essen, Germany	World Team Member
1989	Belgrade, Yugoslavia	World Team Member

Major International Honors

Gold Medals

1987 World Championships	Essen, Germany
1987 Pan American Games	Indianapolis, USA
1991 US Open	
1988 Italian Open	
1984 Belgian Open	
1984 Czechoslovakian Open	
1982 Dutch Open	

Silver Medals

1989 World Championships	Belgrade, Yugoslavia
1985 World Championships	Seoul, Korea
1991 Sungkok Cup	Korea
Pacific Rim Championships	Hawaii
1990 Goodwill Games	Seattle
1987 Shoriki Cup	Japan
1986 Kano Cup	Japan
1985 Matsumae Cup	Austria
1983 & 1985 US Open	Colorado Springs, USA
1977 Pan American Championships	Argentina

About the Author

Bronze Medals

1988 Olympic Games	Seoul, Korea
1989 Pacific Rim Championships	China
1987 German Open	Germany
1985 Pacific Rim Championships	Japan
1984 German Open	Germany
1983 Pan American Games	Caracos, Venezuela
1983 Pacific Rim Championships	Japan
1981 Dutch Open	
1981 US Open	San Jose, USA
1980 US Open	Hartford, USA

National Honors

Gold Medals
5 Time National Champion
4 Time Collegiate Champion
5 Time Olympic Festival Champion

www.ingramcontent.com/pod-product-compliance
Lightning Source LLC
Chambersburg PA
CBHW081346080526
44588CB00016B/2393